T0055015

God: A Very Short Introduction

VERY SHORT INTRODUCTIONS are for anyone wanting a stimulating and accessible way in to a new subject. They are written by experts, and have been translated into more than 40 different languages.

The Series began in 1995, and now covers a wide variety of topics in every discipline. The VSI library now contains over 350 volumes—a Very Short Introduction to everything from Psychology and Philosophy of Science to American History and Relativity—and continues to grow in every subject area.

Very Short Introductions available now:

Available soon:

For more information visit our website

www.oup.com/vsi/

John Bowker

GOD

A Very Short Introduction

OXFORD
UNIVERSITY PRESS

OXFORD
UNIVERSITY PRESS

Great Clarendon Street, Oxford, OX2 6DP,
United Kingdom

Oxford University Press is a department of the University of Oxford.
It furthers the University's objective of excellence in research, scholarship,
and education by publishing worldwide. Oxford is a registered trade mark of
Oxford University Press in the UK and in certain other countries

Published in the United States of America by Oxford University Press
198 Madison Avenue, New York, NY 10016, United States of America

British Library Cataloguing in Publication Data
Data available

Library of Congress Control Number: 2014936250

ISBN 978-0-19-870895-7

Printed and bound by CPI Group (UK) Ltd, Croydon, CR0 4YY

Contents

Preface

Most people throughout history and in all parts of the world have believed in God, as the majority still do. But who or what is it that they believe in? The ways in which people describe God and interact with God are so different that they have led, not just to disagreement, but even to conflict and war. Is God one or many? Is God up there or down here? Is God outside the universe or is the universe the body of God? The variety is so bewildering that any *Introduction to God* has to begin with the question, 'Who or what is God?'

It is a complicated question to answer. Even the word 'God' does not mean the same thing for all people at all times. Should we even use the word 'God'? Why not 'Goddess'? In fact many of the earliest cults and imaginations of Deity thought of her as Goddess, as the Mother who is the source and sustenance of all life. It has even been argued (particularly from archaeological remains) that 'God was female for at least the first 200,000 years of human life on earth'. In India down to the present day Goddesses as well as Gods are recognized and worshipped.

In contrast, in the so-called Abrahamic religions (Judaism, Christianity and Islam), the Deity is overwhelmingly masculine even though traces of the feminine and of God as Mother remain.

In those religions, people use masculine verbs and pronouns to refer to God, and masculinity dominates what they imagine the nature and character of God to be. That basic characterization of God affects very much how they live their lives: women, for example, have not usually, until very recently, been allowed by men to be rabbis, priests, or imams leading mixed-gender congregational prayer.

Should we, then, avoid using the word 'God' and use the word 'Deity' instead? That seems far too artificial, and in any case it obscures the fact that Deity often *is* described as God with masculine characteristics. So in general the word 'God' will be used in this book, but 'the return of the feminine' after centuries of male domination is already affecting our understanding of God. In recognition of this, and as a reminder of its importance, masculine or feminine pronouns in relation to God are not used except in quotations (which for copyright reasons cannot be altered) and in description or discussion of Indian religions where the distinction between masculine and feminine is necessary.

Of course in the end, whatever God is lies far beyond all human words and descriptions, and certainly far beyond gender. But in the meantime we have to recognize that there are a multitude of different descriptions and characterizations of God, some of them bringing gods and goddesses well within the range of human description. We have to recognize also that through time understandings of God do not remain the same. Even within a particular religion, there will be dramatic changes (and often profound disagreements) in the way in which people think and speak about God.

At first sight that may seem a bit surprising. After all, if God is *God*, surely God does not change? That may be so: 'Change and decay in all around I see: O Thou who changest not, abide with me.' Even so, what *do* change are the descriptions and characterizations of God made at different times and in different religions.

Take, as a quick example, the movement from Dyaus to Zeus. In ancient India, the Sky was thought to be the source of life and sustenance (sun and rain) and of sudden destruction (storm and lightning). The Sky as the agent of these effects was called Dyaus. But when the different effects were attributed to separate agents (the Sun became Surya), Dyaus became one of the eight spheres of existence in which the gods and goddesses live. Dyaus meanwhile spread to other lands and became, in Greece, Zeus. Once there, Zeus became the Patriarch of the other gods and goddesses who have been described in the times of Homer (8th century BCE) as 'a bunch of squabbling prima donnas who demand respect and homage from their human followers, and who can turn very nasty if they feel that this respect is not forthcoming.' By the time of Aeschylus (6/5th century BCE), the characterization of Zeus is different: he has become more remote (the opening Chorus of *Agamemnon* declares, 'Zeus, whoever he may be, if this name pleases him in supplication, so I call upon him'), and in the Hymn to Zeus written by the Stoic philosopher Cleanthes (4th/3rd century BCE), Zeus has become the only God who brings into being everything that exists and who guides all creation with the universal Word of Reason.

From that brief example we can see how people in different times and places change greatly their understandings and characterizations of God even when they use the same name or alter it only slightly. The often dramatic developments are not so surprising when we remember how much the human understanding of everything moves on from one generation to another. In the natural sciences, for example, the universe is constantly being understood in new ways which correct the past. In both cases, in the sciences and in the understanding of God, there is certainly much that is *un*changing because it has been tested through time and has been found to be reliable. Even so, there is much that has not stayed the same. It may well be the case that both God and the universe are what they are, but the ways in which we think and speak about them are transformed as we grow in experience, understanding, and wisdom.

This is fundamental in trying to understand God, and it will be illustrated at much greater length in this book. The point is that even if *God* does not change, the ways in which different people and different religions have described and *characterized* God (that is, have given to God a particular nature and character) are vastly different and actually do change through time. The meaning of God is not fixed. Religions and religious believers are often reluctant to accept this, and their reluctance may well arise from feelings of loyalty and faithfulness. And yet their understanding and characterization of God cannot remain the same (no longer does God have a white beard sitting on a throne just above the clouds). In a well-known quotation from *The Leopard*, Falconeri observes, 'If we want things to stay as they are, things will have to change.'

By now it will, I hope, be clear why an *Introduction to God* has to begin by asking to whom or to what we are being introduced. Who or what is God? The most direct answer is to say that 'God' is the word people use when they want to talk about whatever is the ultimate and absolute Reality. Different religions may identify and describe the ultimately Real in different ways, but they are at least at one in believing that there is such Reality 'in its infinite mystery beyond the scope of the human intellect.'

If that is so, then one might conclude that religions are simply different roads leading to the same destination. A problem, however, is that roads do not necessarily lead to the same destination simply by virtue of being roads. Roads can lead in the wrong direction. Religions speak about God in such contradictory and often mutually exclusive ways that they have led to wars, conflict and persecution.

So an *Introduction to God* must look carefully at how and why people in different religions have formed their different and often conflicting beliefs about God. In the major religions of the world, the formative beliefs and practices lie far back in the past. No matter how much those beliefs and practices have been developed and transformed, they remain interpretations and applications of what has been received from the past *with authority*, transmitted in text and tradition. To understand what people believe about God in the present, we have to understand the formative foundations that were laid in the past, and that is why the relevant chapters in this book start so long ago in Canaan and in the Indus Valley.

So who or what is God?

Chapter 1 looks at ways in which philosophers and theologians have tried to answer that question in careful and precise language. In contrast, poets and believers use far more vivid and descriptive language to speak *of* God and to speak *to* God in prayer and worship. How are the two 'languages' related to each other? And do they tell us the truth? That question leads in Chapter 1 to a consideration of some of the major arguments for and against God, and to the reason why the arguments often lead to judgements of probability and not to conclusive demonstration.

Chapter 2 turns to the question of why people believe in God. Some examples are given of the many different answers that have been offered to that question. What is important for many believers is the consequence of God in life and in experience. What that experience means and how it is related to recent research in the neurosciences is then explored.

Chapters 3, 4, 5, and 6 look at particular religions in more detail in order to see what all this means in religious life and practice. A short book cannot summarize all that has been believed about God in all the religions of the world. Instead, two different groups of religions will be looked at in more detail, the so-called Abrahamic religions (Judaism, Christianity and Islam) and those of India. The focus in each case will be, *first*, on the way in which their very different characterizations and descriptions of God came to be established, and then, *second*, on the way in which the first and foundational characterizations began to be, from the earliest days, developed and transformed. Again for reasons of space, the later developments cannot be described, although some reference is given to them. This is not, and cannot be, a history of religions. In the final chapter, the vital question is asked, 'How can God be known?'

Acknowledgements

Some of this book has been written by my wife, Margaret, who is in a measure the co-author of it. Because of my increasingly limited eyesight, she has also corrected it with great care, but remaining mistakes are of course my own responsibility. I owe an immense debt of gratitude to her for that and for so much more. Both of us are equally grateful for the help and encouragement offered by Sarah Brunning.

My thanks go as well to many people who helped with suggestions and corrections, and in particular to Peter Barrett, Chip Coakley, Quinton Deeley, David Hay, Ben O'Rourke OSA, and Romie Ridley. I am especially grateful to Dr Viswanathan for supplying his own portrayal of Mahadevi, and to Gavin Flood without whose support it is unlikely that the book would have been published. My thanks also go to Gary Wade and the 6th Form at St John's School, Leatherhead, who took time after exams to read an early draft: their comments were extremely helpful.

A particular word of thanks must go to the many involved at Oxford University Press. The process turned out to be far more complicated than anyone had expected, and as a result, the commissioning editor, Andrea Keegan, was involved in much extra work. I am grateful to her for her skill in general and her patience under pressure. It was a pleasure also to work with Emma Ma, Carol Carnegie, Carrie Hickman, Joy Mellor, and Kay Clement, and I thank them for their skill and help.

God

Note on transliteration

In this book the transliteration of other languages is not precise. It does not, for example, include any of the diacritical marks except in quotations. Thus Śiva appears as Shiva. There is a particular problem in Arabic. The Arabic word for 'the' is *al*, and it is attached to its noun. Thus 'the house' is in Arabic *albait*. A widespread convention in transliterating Arabic inserts a hyphen between *al* and the following noun, hence *al-bait*. That, however, is unhelpful and misleading because it obliterates the distinction between two different groups of letters in the Arabic alphabet, the 14 so-called 'sun letters' (in contrast to the 'moon letters') where the letter *l* of *al* merges with the first letter of the noun. Thus 'the sun' is *ashshams*, not *alshams*. Authors who know Arabic respect this (as does, for example, Chittick in the Further Reading, at the end of this book), but it creates problems in the alphabetical order of an index. I have therefore adopted a compromise between the unhelpful convention and the proper respect for Arabic: for the 'sun letters' I have inserted a hyphen between the article and the noun (e.g., *al-shams*), and for the 'moon letters' I have followed Arabic usage and attached the article to the noun (e.g., *alQuran*). So, for example, two Meccan deities appear as alUzza and al-Lat (the letter l being one of the 'sun letters').

List of illustrations

Chapter 1
Does God exist?

> The White Rabbit put on his spectacles. 'Where shall I
> begin, please your Majesty?' he asked.
>
> 'Begin at the beginning,' the King said gravely, 'and go on till
> you come to the end, then stop.'

We, on the other hand, will have to do almost exactly the opposite:
we will have to begin at the end, go on till we stop, then find that it
is, after all, only the beginning.

To start, then, at the end: before we can be introduced to God, it
would be a big help if we could have some idea of who or what it is
that we are being introduced to. So who or what is God?

Speaking of God: philosophers and poets

Countless answers to that question have been given during the
long course of human history, some expressed in practical ways like
sacrifice and worship, others in reflective ways like those of
theology and philosophy, or in imaginative ways like art and music.
Each of us perhaps has a personal answer already, including maybe
that God is not anything because God does not exist.

That particular answer (that God does not exist) is one reason why
the reflective ways of theology and philosophy have come into

being. Philosophers and theologians respond to questions asked about God, not only to the question, 'Does God exist?', but also to such questions as, 'If God is supposed to be all-powerful (omnipotent) and all-loving, why is there so much suffering and evil?'; or, 'If God is believed to be omniscient (knowing everything including what I choose to do), is my "choice" real since its outcome is already known?'

There are a multitude of other questions asked about God: is God a person? Does God answer prayer? If so, how? Is God one or many? Fundamentally, however, philosophers and theologians try to make clear what God would have to be for God to be truly *God*—to be, that is, the One from whom the universe comes and by whom it is kept in being. What would God have to be in order to do all that and to be truly worthy of the sacrifice and worship that humans have offered for so long in so many different ways?

God, to repeat the point, has been described in many ways in the long history of religions, and the word 'God' has had many different meanings. God has been defined as 'that than which nothing greater can be thought of' and as 'a circle whose centre is everywhere and whose circumference is nowhere'. At the opposite extreme the actress Jane Russell described God as 'a livin' doll, a right nice guy' and Chesterton wrote:

> Some see God like Guthrum,
> Crowned, with a great beard curled,
> But I see God like a good giant
> That labouring lifts the world.

When, as a boy, Augustine (a Christian bishop and teacher, 354–430 CE) prayed to God he thought of God as 'some large being who, although not apparent to our senses, is able to hear us and to help us.' God has often been described like that, in human terms, as someone very like ourselves but on a much higher level—as Mother, for example, or as King. That is not surprising, for how else could God be imagined? The French philosopher Montesquieu (1689–1755) once observed that if triangles had a God, God would have three sides; and his near contemporary Voltaire (1694–1778) commented on *Genesis* 1.27 ('God made man in his image'), 'God made man in his own image and man has more than returned the compliment.'

For philosophers and theologians, it has been a major part of their work to examine and question to what extent, if any, those descriptions are adequate, and where they fail. More positively, they are asking what God must be once we realize that God is not 'someone very like ourselves but a bit bigger'. Over thousands of years, they have addressed the issue of what we can truly or (in terms of logic and argument) validly say about God.

As a result, they have ended up with definitions of what the word 'God' must mean if it is to have a truly significant sense. Definitions of what God must be in order to be *God* cannot of course demonstrate that God exists, but they are nevertheless important because they track the rigour of human thought in relation to God, and they at least give us a first idea of who or what it is that we are being introduced to.

That is why this book is beginning where the long history of philosophy and theology has, thus far, ended up. We are beginning at the end in order that we can see from the outset where the long history of the intellectual and reflective response to God has been leading. What is it that we are trying to talk about? Or to put the question slightly differently, in the words of the contemporary philosopher Richard Swinburne:

> How is the claim that there is a God to be understood? I suggest—
> provisionally—in this way: there exists necessarily and eternally
> a person essentially bodiless, omnipresent, creator and sustainer of
> any universe there may be, perfectly free, omnipotent, omniscient,
> perfectly good, and a source of moral obligation.

1. Daily prayer, Salat, facing Mecca is an obligation for Muslims even alone in the desert. Words and postures are laid down. The bowing (*ruku*) is made while saying (three times), 'Glory to God the Mighty'

But if that is where we are going to end up, are we sure that we want to get there? It sounds very different from Indian villagers shaping images in clay and adorning them with flowers, or from Muslims turning five times each day towards Mecca and offering prayer (see Figure 1), or from Sikh mothers placing a drop of honey on the tongue of a new-born child and whispering in its ear the Mul Mantra.

Such people have been a vast majority throughout human history, as they still are. For them God is simply there, the one in whose presence and company they live, often in an undramatic way, but on occasion with a very direct sense of vision and encounter. They have found (without necessarily thinking too much about it) that God gives meaning and purpose to their lives as well as strength and support in times of trouble.

The poet Les Murray tried to capture this sense of the constant presence of God when he wrote that God is in the world as the poetry is in the poem—echoing another poet, Campantar from S. India (7th/8th century CE), who wrote that God is of constant effect in the world as the sense is within speech. But here the gap between the philosophers and the poets seems extremely wide. When a poet and psalmist asked the question, 'Who is the King of glory?', the answer given was very different from that of the philosopher: 'It is the Lord strong and mighty, even the Lord mighty in battle..., even the Lord of hosts, he is the King of glory.' How can that vivid sense of God be related to the God of the philosophers? How can 'a person essentially bodiless' be mighty in battle, smiting enemies and 'killing mighty kings'? How, in India, can a source of moral obligation slaughter her consort Shiva and dance naked on his corpse as does the bloodthirsty Kali, the embodiment of the destructive energy of Time? When the French philosopher and mathematician, Pascal (1623–62) felt that he had a direct experience of God it was like a burning fire far removed from the God of philosophical reflection:

> The year of grace 1654...
> From about half past ten at night until about half past midnight,
> FIRE.
> GOD of Abraham, GOD of Isaac, GOD of Jacob
> not of the philosophers and of the learned.
> Certitude. Certitude. Feeling. Joy. Peace....

Pascal's experience seemed to him far removed from philosophers thinking and writing about God. And yet, if we are hoping to be 'introduced to God', as the title of this book suggests, we have to ask how the two are connected. How is the widely-claimed experience of God (fire and certitude, joy and peace) related to the careful and thoughtful reflection of the philosophers and theologians? Or to put it the other way round, why have the philosophers ended up defining God as 'necessarily and eternally a person essentially bodiless' and so on, where believers have simply bowed their heads in adoration and prayer?

The two are most obviously related by the fact that both the believers and the philosophers are using words and language to speak in different ways about the same subject matter—namely, God. Believers speak to God and speak of God in whatever words and languages are available to them in their own place and time; they even include sounds that lie beyond the words of everyday use as, for example, in mantras or in what is known in Christianity as 'speaking in tongues'. Philosophers consider the words and the claims that underlie them, and they ask what the underlying claims imply, and whether they can be expressed truly or validly in a more detached way.

How the two are related can be seen, by way of example, in the words of two poems from very different times and places, Psalm 24 (from which came the question above, 'Who is the King of glory?') and 'Marumat tirut tantakam' of Appar (7th century in South India). The words are vivid and personal, and yet they point to the more dispassionate and abstract conclusions of the philosophers: the two belong together. Psalm 24 begins:

> The earth is the Lord's, and all that therein is: the compass of the
>   world, and they that dwell therein.
> For he hath founded it upon the seas: and prepared it upon the
>   floods.
> Who shall ascend into the hill of the Lord: or who shall rise up in
>   his holy place?
> Even he that hath clean hands, and a pure heart: and that hath not
>   lift up his mind unto vanity, nor sworn to deceive his neighbour.
> He shall receive the blessing from the Lord: and righteousness from
>   the God of his salvation.

That is a poetic way of speaking of God as 'creator and sustainer of any universe there may be, perfectly good, and a source of moral obligation' (as Swinburne put it), but it has done so in the words of one who is approaching the Temple in Jerusalem in order to worship God. Similarly vs.7 of Appar's poem speaks of God as 'eternally a person, omnipresent, perfectly free, omnipotent, omniscient, and perfectly good', but it does so in the language of a devoted lover:

> Our sole duty is joyfully to sing
> the glory of him who manifests himself
> as the moving and the still,
> as earth, water, fire, wind, and sky,
> as the small and the great,
> as hard to reach, yet easily attained
> by his lovers,
> as the highest reality, immeasurably great,
> as infinite Sadāśiva, as you and me.

Words and meanings

With reference to God, therefore, philosophers and believers are using words and language in their own very different ways in order to say something about (or, in the case of believers, something to) God. But what are they talking about? To what if anything are they referring?

In the case of God, it is clear that they cannot be referring to any *thing* that can be found among the many things in the universe. If God is the Creator and the sustainer of every-*thing*, the Creator and sustainer of this or any other universe, then God cannot be a part of what has been created. God is not an object among the many objects in the universe.

This means that God cannot be produced for inspection like a rare animal, nor can we be introduced to God as we might be to a stranger. Think, for example, of Mr Pickwick at Manor Farm in Kent:

> Several guests who were assembled in the old parlour rose to greet
> Mr Pickwick and his friends upon their entrance; and during the

performance of the ceremony of introduction, with all the
formalities, Mr Pickwick had leisure to observe the appearance, and
speculate upon the characters and pursuits, of the persons by whom
he was surrounded—a habit in which he in common with many
other great men delighted to indulge.

God is not like a person in Kent whose appearance can be observed
and recognized in that way. Similarly, God is not here today and
gone tomorrow in the way that you and I happen to be here now
but may not be so tomorrow. To use the technical word, we are
contingent, a part of time and circumstance, but if God is the source
of all that is contingent, God is *not* contingent. God simply *is*.

Only if that is so, and God is not contained as we are within the
conditions of space and time, can God be the One from whom
space and time (and indeed all things) take their being and by
whom they are kept in being: God to be *God* must be the
unproduced Producer of all that is. Or as Aquinas (1225–74; a
Christian philosopher and theologian) put it: 'God is to be thought
of as existing outside the domain of existents, as a cause from
whom comes everything that exists in all its different forms'.

It follows that there is a serious sense in which we have to say that
God does not *exist* because otherwise we would be placing God
among things that might or might not exist. That is why Kierkegaard
(1813–55, the Danish philosopher often regarded as a father of
modern existentialism) could say, 'God does not exist, he is eternal.'

On the other hand, we can equally say that *only* God truly exists
because all creatures have their moment of existence in time but
they have no reality outside time: they come into being and cease
to be. By coming into being they are caused to exist, but God is not
caused in that or any other way.

There is here an important but difficult distinction. In the case of
all contingent beings (like a human or a hamster) we can know

what essentially a human is and what therefore distinguishes humans from hamsters. But that knowledge of *essence* does not tell us whether a particular human happens to *exist*. We know what it means to be a unicorn or a phoenix (i.e., what they essentially are), but it does not follow that any phoenix or any unicorn actually exists.

In contrast, to be God is, at least by definition, to exist. God to be God, the unproduced Producer of all that is, cannot be dependent for existence on anyone or anything else. In other words, it has to belong logically to the definition (and actuality) of God that God does not derive existence from any other things or beings, but must necessarily be the One whose essence is simply to be.

On that basis it makes obvious sense for believers to 'put their trust in God', for nothing else can be as trustworthy. So when Muslims, for example, put their trust in God and enter into that condition of obedience and safety which is the meaning of the word *islam*, they entrust themselves to One who simply *is*, no matter whether this or any other universe happens to come into being or to an end. Their 'safety', in other words, is not vulnerable because it rests on One who sustains but does not need sustenance. God *transcends* this or any other universe (i.e., God is Transcendent). As the Quran (6.14) challenges the believer:

> Say: shall I take for my protector any other than God, the maker of the heavens and the earth? He it is that feeds but is not fed.

But if God as Creator is so transcendently other and so distinct from all that has been created, how can we speak about God at all? Philosophers and theologians may try to define what God would have to be if the word 'God' is to be used in an adequate and non-trivial way. But if we then speak of God as Creator, do we mean that God is like a potter making a pot as the Jewish and the Christian Bibles say (*Isaiah* 64.8; *Job* 18.6; *Romans* 9.21)? If the description were taken literally, it would imply that God sits down at a wheel and shapes the earth like a pot out of clay. But that would make God as limited and contingent as we are, having a body and hands with which to make things.

Or again, when the Quran (earlier) says that God is 'the maker' of the heavens and the earth, the Arabic verb used is *fatara*. That verb can mean 'he split open', 'he baked unleavened bread', 'he milked a ewe with thumb and forefinger', 'he had breakfast'. None of those meanings can be applied literally to God as the Creator of the heavens and the earth.

It is clear, therefore, that we cannot use words about God in exactly the same way, and with the same sense, as we use them of the world in which we live. We cannot use words *univocally* to mean of God what we mean by them in everyday life.

On the other hand, the words we use of God must have *some* connection with the words of everyday life because otherwise we cannot know what they might mean. We would be using words in two entirely different senses, as, for example, when we use the word 'hide' for the skin of an animal or for a place of concealment. 'Hide' in that example is being used *equivocally* in two unconnected senses.

So if we cannot speak of God either univocally (because the Creator, the unproduced Producer of all that is, is necessarily different from all that has been created) or equivocally (because that would make the Creator unintelligibly different from what has been created), then how can we speak of God at all?

Speaking of God: analogy, omnipotence and omniscience

The classic answer has been to say that we can speak of God by analogy. There is a relatedness between the Creator and creation in the sense that creation is the consequence of what the Creator intended and keeps in being. If, therefore, we can say that a bridge is strong, that a heavy-weight boxer is strong, that a beer is strong, we can by analogy understand what is indicated when we say that 'God is strong and mighty in battle'. We are not saying that God is a high-alcohol intoxicant (univocal) or that God's strength has no connection at all with our own rich and varied understandings of 'strength' (equivocal), but rather that we gain some insight into God's 'omnipotence' when we reflect on the human understandings of what it means to be strong (analogy). God is strong but not exactly as we use the word 'strong' of ourselves or of objects in the universe: the claim that God is omnipotent means that God can do everything that is *logically* possible (or physio-logically or any other of the '-logically possibles') but even God cannot create a four-sided triangle.

Do miracles contradict that? Only if a miracle is defined as something that is not -logically possible but has nevertheless occurred. There are of course stories about miracles of that kind, but they remain stories of the impossible, and as stories they can still be instructive because truths can be told as much through fiction as through fact—even if it is, as the poet George Herbert put it, 'catching the sense at two removes'.

In contrast, however, the word 'miracle' comes from the Latin word, *miror*, 'I marvel at', 'I am amazed'. In that sense, there is much that is miraculous, and it is certainly true that God can 'omnipotently' do things long before humans can do the same. Healings are a good example: some that are claimed to have happened in the past and were thought at the time to be otherwise impossible, have now through surgery and medicine become a commonplace, but they remain just as miraculous in the sense that they amaze and astonish us—provided, of course, that we do not simply take them for granted.

Similar considerations apply to 'omniscience': God cannot know anything that is not available to be known, such as the name of a barren woman's son (to quote the example from India in Chapter 6). Another more practical example lies in the fact that in a post-quantum world, some future events cannot be known beyond probability—in contrast to a post-Newtonian belief that the future can be predicted (at least in principle) from the present. 'The Newtonian universe', as Manjit Kumar has put it, 'is purely deterministic with no room for chance.... Probability was a consequence of human ignorance in any deterministic universe where everything unfolded according to the laws of nature.'

Until very recently, therefore, 'probability' was thought to be a figleaf with which to cover our temporary ignorance so that, as science advances, probability would be replaced by certainty. Thus it was believed that an omniscient being would know the present state and momentum of all the atoms in the universe and could therefore deduce all future outcomes. As Huxley (Darwin's bulldog, 1825–95) observed of John Tyndall:

> A favourite problem of his is—Given the molecular forces in a mutton chop, deduce Hamlet or Faust therefrom. He is confident that the Physics of the Future will solve this easily.

In that Newtonian world it was thought that the certainties achieved by scientific progress would drive ignorance into retreat and banish the tentative guesswork of probability. Now it is different. In fact (in a post-quantum world) it is clear that neither God nor for that matter any supercomputer can dispense with *probability* since it is inherent in the universe, and that therefore there are free actions in the future which are not available to be known. One of Feynman's 'first principles of quantum mechanics' states, 'the only thing that can be predicted is the probability of different events'. For reasons of that kind God has been defined more correctly as being omniscient

> if and only if it is impossible for there to be a being with greater cognitive power and this power is fully exercised.... [S]o long as

God

12

God's cognitive power is unsurpassable, and it is fully exercised, God's not knowing future free acts does not compromise God being omniscient.

Both those examples (omnipotence and omniscience) illustrate the highly qualified basis on which analogy enables us to speak of God. There are then two different types of analogy. In the first, a word that applies to one thing is applied to another, as when we say that a person is healthy and then apply that word by analogy to a bank balance: strictly speaking, only the living organism can be healthy, but we know what we mean when we call a bank balance 'healthy' (that kind of analogy is known technically as 'the analogy of attribution').

In the second kind of analogy, a word is used that applies in both cases but in different ways, as when we say of a person and of a plant that each is 'living'. It is true of both, but what it means to be living is not identical in the two cases: both possess the relevant characteristic, but each possesses it in relation or proportion to its own nature (that kind of analogy is known as 'the analogy of proportionality').

Atheism

Both kinds of analogy can be applied to God, though not without caution and often in the face of contest and dissent. If, for example, we say that God is love but not exactly in the ways in which we understand love, the 'not exactly' may take so much away that we are left with nothing. The philosopher Antony Flew called it 'death by a thousand qualifications':

Someone tells us that God loves us as a father loves his children. We are reassured. But then we see a child dying of inoperable cancer of the throat. His earthly father is driven frantic in his efforts to help, but his Heavenly Father reveals no obvious sign of concern. Some qualification is made—God's love is 'not a merely human love' or it is 'an inscrutable love', perhaps—and we realise that such sufferings are quite compatible with the truth of the assertion that 'God loves us as a father (but, of course,….).' We are reassured again. But then perhaps we ask: what is this assurance of God's (appropriately qualified) love worth,…? Just what would have to happen not merely (morally and wrongly) to tempt but also (logically and rightly) to entitle us to say 'God does not love us' or even 'God does not exist'?

In Flew's perception, claims about God are qualified so much that 'God' fades away like the grin of the Cheshire cat: 'A fine brash hypothesis may thus be killed by inches, the death by a thousand qualifications.' We may empty a bath one cup at a time and each cup may seem to make little difference, but we end up with an empty bath.

If that is so, then it would seem impossible to say anything significant about God at all, and some have therefore concluded that the only option is to be an atheist (Greek *a*, 'not' + *theos*, 'god'). That is exactly the conclusion that Flew came to himself, writing a book called *The Presumption of Atheism* in which he argued that the use of the word 'God' must be defined or given a meaning that would make it possible (even if only in theory) for an actual being to be described in that way. If we define God as a four-sided triangle, no amount of argument will ever produce, even in theory, an actual entity to be described in that way. In the view of Flew (at that time) and of many others, to define 'God' as 'a bodiless person' is closer to a four-sided triangle then it is to an actual entity.

The difficulty of using words and language to speak about God as traditionally understood, as Being utterly transcendent, led many during the 20th century to abandon the tradition and to redefine God in terms of this world. Prominent among them was Dietrich Bonhoeffer (a German Lutheran pastor, 1906–45) who argued that the traditional understanding is indefensible:

The god hypothesis is no longer of any pragmatic value for the interpretation or comprehension of nature, and indeed often stands in the way of better and truer interpretation. Operationally, God is beginning to resemble not a ruler but the last fading smile of a cosmic Cheshire cat....

It will soon be as impossible for an intelligent, educated man or woman to believe in a God as it is now to believe that the earth is flat, that flies can be spontaneously generated, that disease is a divine punishment, or that death is always due to witchcraft. Gods will doubtless survive, sometimes under the protection of vested interests, or in the shelter of lazy minds, or as puppets used by politicians, or as refuges for unhappy and ignorant souls.

As a result, Bonhoeffer called for 'the abandonment of a false conception of God in a world come of age' which brings God into the universe from outside it in order to explain the gaps in our knowledge or understanding—the so-called 'God of the gaps'. But Bonhoeffer did not abandon God and become an atheist—indeed, his beliefs about what in practice 'costly discipleship' must mean, led to his execution by the Nazis in 1945. He claimed that we have to find God in what we know, not in what we do not know, and he defined God as 'the Beyond in the midst of life'. Instead of the Transcendent God far above and beyond us, the effective meaning of God has to be found here dwelling in our midst—or, to use the word that corresponds to Transcendence, God has to be recognized as *Immanent* (from the Latin *in* + *manere*, 'to dwell within', 'to remain').

The death of God: transcendence and immanence

Following Bonhoeffer's example, others in the period after the Second World War declared that 'God is dead'—though many others, including Jains and Buddhists in Asia, had pronounced the death of God more than two thousand years earlier. In the West, Nietzsche stated in 1887 that the death of God was a recent event, but long before that (according to Cicero) Diagoras had chopped up a statue of Heracles in order to boil his turnips and had proclaimed outright that God does not exist.

One consequence of 'the death of God' as pronounced in the 20th century was an exploration of what the word 'God' might mean if it is redefined in terms of Immanence. For example, instead of attempts to defend the traditional understanding of the Transcendence of God, the meaning of God was reconstructed from the ways in which people experience Nature or the laws of Nature as an independent and omnipotent power in the universe controlling our destiny.

The redefining of God in terms of Nature went back in part to the beginning of the scientific revolution in the 17th century, and in particular to the philosopher Spinoza (1633–77). He argued that 'God' is the single and only infinite substance and is therefore equivalent to Nature—'that eternal and infinite Being that we call God or nature', a view usually summarized in the words *Deus sive Natura*. It is thus a form of pantheism (from the Greek *pan*, 'everything' + *theos*, 'god').

Spinoza made God as Immanent as any account of God can be—and Spinoza was expelled from the Amsterdam synagogue because 'Deus sive Natura' obliterated the radical distinction in Judaism between a Transcendent Creator and what has been created. His views, however, gave powerful impetus to later attempts to redefine 'God' within the universe, not least in his distinction between Nature as it is observed from the outside and Nature as the process through which all things come into being and develop.

The focus on *process* became the foundation of the work of the philosopher and mathematician, A. N. Whitehead (1861–1947) whose attempt to redefine God within the universe rather than lapse into atheism was widely influential, and was indeed called Process Theology. He started even further back than Spinoza with some words from Plato's *Timaeus*, claiming that 'everything is always in the process of becoming and perishing and never really is'. Whitehead held that the universe is made up, not of permanently enduring 'things', but of interacting 'occasions of experience' directed towards the realization of what gives them value. The whole system is within God (hence it is known as 'panentheism' in contrast to pantheism) who is the guarantee of order and the unlimited potentiality that allows actualities to occur, and who draws them towards their final completion and satisfaction. God is the attraction or, in Whitehead's word, 'the lure' that draws every possibility into its completion.

The stress on Immanence did not, of course, begin with philosophical dilemmas in the 20th century. According to E. B. Tylor (1832–1917; a key figure in establishing anthropology as an academic discipline), Immanence in the form of Animism is the origin of religion itself. Animism (from the Latin *anima*, 'soul' or 'spirit') is the belief that all natural living things are animated by a super-natural Spirit that can be interacted with in various rituals of recognition—many of which continue to the present day. So Tylor claimed that 'animism is, in fact, the ground work of the Philosophy of Religion, from that of savages up to that of civilised men'.

Tylor's speculation about origins is implausible, but animistic beliefs are certainly widespread, and they serve as a reminder that variations on the theme of Immanence are fundamental in all religions and paramount in some. For example, the Kami in Japan are the sacred and spiritual powers venerated by the Japanese, but in a way that cannot be equated with (or translated as) God in a Transcendent sense. There are 'vast myriads of Kami' pervading the entire universe and giving to objects and to humans their characteristic strength and style. Humans recognize and interact with them in many ways including offerings and prayers at shrines or in the home, but the Kami are worshipped for what they are, and not as manifestations of a transcendent God.

Those two examples of Immanence (Animism and the Kami) remain well within the traditional religious world. Bonhoeffer's call for 'religionless Christianity' was looking for a translation of traditional religious language into a secular (*saeculum*, 'belonging to this age' or 'this world') vocabulary of values. Paul Tillich (1886–1965, an American philosopher and theologian) was a well-known advocate and exponent of this, particularly when his views were given striking expression in John Robinson's *Honest to God* (1963). Tillich claimed that the word 'God' is needed to refer to the absolute and unshakeable foundation of our lives, the ground of our being, the depth of our seriousness about the worth and meaning of life:

> The name of this infinite and inexhaustible depth and ground of all being is *God*. That depth is what the word *God* means…. [I]f you know that God means depth, you know much about him. You cannot then call yourself an atheist or unbeliever. For you cannot think or say: 'Life has no depth! Life is shallow. Being itself is surface only.' If you could say this in complete seriousness, you would be an atheist; but otherwise you are not. He who knows about depth knows about God.

But does he—or she? In the long and world-wide traditions of the past, the great pioneers and explorers of the human relationship with God could say with just as much conviction that God is the ground of our being and our ultimate concern, but they discovered that that truly 'unshakeable foundation' is far more personally engaged with us and a great deal more profound than our feelings about depth. Thus to give only one example, John Ruusbroec (1293–1381; his name often appears as Ruysbroeck) wrote, 'The Father is our ground and origin in which we begin our being and our life.' The difference is that Ruusbroec used the word 'Father' which points (analogically) to relationship, to what he called 'an active meeting'. For that to develop into 'a blissful embrace of loving immersion' as Ruusbroec and many others have experienced it, the Transcendence of God, far beyond the power

God

18

of words to describe, is the literal *sine qua non*, 'that without which' it cannot occur *as it does*:

> Now this active meeting and this loving embrace are in their ground blissful and devoid of particular form, for the fathomless, modeless being of God is so dark and so devoid of particular form that it encompasses within itself all the divine modes and the activity and properties of the Persons in the rich embrace of the essential Unity; it thereby produces a divine state of blissful enjoyment in this abyss of the ineffable. Here there is a blissful crossing over and a self-transcending immersion into a state of essential bareness.... Here there is nothing other than an eternal state of rest in a blissful embrace of loving immersion. This is that modeless being which all fervent interior spirits have chosen above all things, that dark stillness in which all lovers lose their way. But if we could prepare ourselves through virtue in the ways I have shown, we would at once strip ourselves of our bodies and flow into the wild waves of the Sea, from which no creature could ever draw us back.

Those are words struggling to say something of the unforgettable experience of God, the experience of falling, not just *in* love, but *into* love, falling into God who is love, an experience to which all are invited and none are compelled.

But words or phrases like 'ineffable' and 'modeless being' infuriate those who ask what we are talking about in the case of God. That is why Flew contended (to use his word) that 'the propounder of a God hypothesis must begin, as would the propounder of any existential hypothesis, by first explaining the particular concept of God to be employed and then indicating how the corresponding object is to be identified.' That is why we have begun in this book by looking at ways in which the concept of God has been articulated.

The dilemma begins when 'the particular concept of God to be employed' maintains that if God is to be *God*, then God has to be defined, as a matter of logical necessity, as Transcendent so that God cannot be produced as an object among other objects in the universe. It is impossible, therefore, to speak about God univocally, and phrases like 'ineffable', 'completely uncomprehended', and 'beyond description' are bound to be used.

But why use them at all? Why not simply accept the argument that the concept of God as Transcendent in that absolute way is not simply 'uncomprehended', it is incomprehensible? That brings us to the other part of Flew's challenge when he asked what *grounds* there are for being theists—for believing that there is a God:

> To believe there is a God, we have to have good grounds for the belief. But if no such grounds are provided, there exists no sufficient reason for believing in God, and the only reasonable position is to be a negative atheist or an agnostic....

Can such 'grounds for belief' be provided? Arguments for God are certainly offered, as much in the present as in the past. Flew's question therefore remains: do any of those arguments provide sufficient reason for believing in God?

Arguments that point to God

Classic arguments in the past are associated particularly with Udayana (*c.*11th century?) in India, and with Thomas Aquinas (1225–74) in the West. In *Nyayakusamanjali* Udayana defended (particularly against Buddhist objections) the view that God exists, is the unproduced Producer of all that is, and is thus responsible for creating, maintaining and destroying the universe. Thomas Aquinas put forward five arguments (known from their summarized form as the Five Ways, or in Latin *Quinque Viae*) on the basis of which he held that reason can be led by argument to know conclusively *that* God is.

Some of their arguments arise from reflections on the universe. They understood the universe very differently from each other and from us, but that does not affect the form or logic of their arguments. Thus they argue that God is required logically and necessarily to explain how the universe has come into being and why it continues as it does ('the cosmological argument'), and also that the universe as a whole and in its parts exhibits a purposeful and intended design which demands the existence of a designer ('the teleological argument', from Greek *telos*, 'end' or 'purpose', often called 'the argument from design' or '*to* design'). The ontological argument moves from a definition of God as perfect being to the conclusion that God therefore must exist. Such arguments are independent of what happens to be known about the universe at any particular time.

Those arguments have persisted even though, through centuries of searching and often acute debate, they have been challenged, corrected and extended. Other arguments have been put forward which are more closely connected to the ways in which we observe and experience the universe. In addition to the cosmological and teleological arguments, Swinburne offers a further four arguments from observed and experienced phenomena that point to the existence of God: arguments from consciousness and morality; from providence; from history and miracles; and from religious experience.

It is not possible in a short introduction to follow or to summarize those long-running arguments 'for and against'. What they share in common is a belief that human reason can discern truth and untruth, and that provided reason is followed wherever it leads (hence the arguments for and against), and provided the arguments are persuasive, it is rational to believe in God (Flew's challenge). Since those arguments make it clear that God cannot be an object among other objects in the universe, then no argument can produce God as something or someone that we can observe and describe. Arguments cannot produce God to be observed and described in the way that the strangers at Manor Farm could be produced for Mr Pickwick 'to observe their appearances'. Nevertheless, what they can do is show why it is rational to accept logical conclusions that have not yet been controverted, and also to accept that our observations and experiences of the universe and of each other point to God as a more probable or more likely explanation of their occurrence than any other.

Observation and inference

Arguments based on what we observe and experience of the universe and of each other infer, or suggest, what is most likely to account for what we observe and experience. Such arguments are known technically as retroductive or abductive inferences. The names may sound too remote and technical to be of much interest to ordinary people. But in fact 'abductive inference' is inescapably important, not just in the sciences, but also in our everyday lives.

Take a look first at sciences. It is often claimed of the sciences that they are based on empirical observations and tests (on what we can actually observe and on repeatable experiments). That is true so far as it goes. But science then has to go further because not all the questions that scientists ask can be answered by simply 'taking a look'. Often something has to be 'abductively inferred' (Latin *ab+ducere*, 'to lead away from') from what is known and has so far been observed. Attempts can then be made to find or to establish whatever it is that has been 'abductively inferred'. A classic example is the way in which Kepler inferred abductively the elliptical path of Mars from its empirically observed irregularities in movement. An equally spectacular example was the announcement in July 2012 that evidence had been found for the Higgs boson (the 'goddamn particle', mischievously and misleadingly abbreviated to 'the god particle') which had been inferred 50 years earlier in order to account for the mass of particles. The very name of the particle 'boson' points to another example. S. N. Bose (1894–1974) was a brilliant physicist whose early work on quantum mechanics (recognized by Einstein) led to Bose-Einstein statistics and the foundation of quantum statistics. The class of particles that obey Bose-Einstein statistics were called 'bosons' by Paul Dirac; and Bose himself inferred and predicted the state of matter of a macroscopic number of free bosons at extremely low temperatures now known as the Bose-Einstein condensate, but its abductively inferred existence was not demonstrated until 1995.

Abductive inference is clearly indispensable in the sciences as it is also in everyday life. We have no choice but to rely on inferences that we draw from our observations and experience. How else, for example, might you know, except by abductive inference from experience, whether the claim of someone to love you is true or well-founded?

Of course the inference you draw, in life or in science, might be wrong, and that is the risk of abductive arguments: they take what is known and ask what is likely to have brought it into being or to what further conclusions it points. In other words, abductive arguments form hypotheses that might be wrong and that can only be held tentatively and with an element of risk. They require, therefore, commitments of trust and faith that the universe is consistently reliable, that people can mean what they say.

On that basis, it is entirely rational and logical to infer abductively, from the observed and experienced universe, that God is the most probable cause of its being. Such arguments, as Swinburne puts it in *The Existence of God*, have a common characteristic:

> They all purport to be arguments to an explanation of the phenomena described in the premisses in terms of the action of an agent who intentionally brought about those phenomena. A cosmological argument argues from the existence of the world to a person, God, who intentionally brought it about. An argument from

design argues from the design of the world to a person, God, who intentionally made it thus. All the other arguments are arguments from particular features of the world to a God who intentionally made the world with those features.

But that inferred 'hypothesis', like other abductively inferred hypotheses, can only be held as at best probable, not as incontrovertibly conclusive (bearing in mind that, as we have just seen, 'probability' is no longer another word for ignorance). That is why Swinburne's book begins with a chapter on inductive arguments and on what probability theory actually involves, and it ends with a chapter entitled 'The Balance of Probability'. Like other abductive arguments, as in the sciences, it requires commitments of trust and faith.

With all that in mind, we can return to Flew's question and challenge: do any of those arguments provide sufficient reason for making that commitment and for believing in God?

According to Flew himself, the answer is, Yes. From a presumption of atheism, he saw instead that there are rational and logical arguments leading to the conclusion that God is, as well as others making it more *probable* that God exists than otherwise. Consequently he published a book in 2007 with the title, *There Is a God: How the World's Most Notorious Atheist Changed His Mind*. What persuaded him to change his mind were the logical and rational arguments, together with the abductively inferential arguments from the universe as it is, which point to God. So he wrote:

> Science qua science cannot furnish an argument for God's existence. But the three items of evidence we have considered—the laws of nature, life with its teleological organization, and the existence of the universe—can only be explained in the light of an Intelligence that explains both its own existence and that of the

world. Such a discovery of the Divine does not come through experiments and equations, but through an understanding of the structures they unveil and map.

Such arguments (of which those of Udayana and Aquinas are examples) are independent of scientific knowledge which is constantly changing. On the other hand, changes in science may reinforce the probability of God (or for that matter diminish it). For example, the argument from order to design has been reinforced by a recognition of how extremely 'fine-tuned' the universe has to be in order for there to be conscious life, and this has produced what is known as 'the anthropic principle': the laws of nature explored in physics combined with certain fixed parameters known as fundamental constants are so precise that only very slight alterations would mean that no life would be possible. The universe turns out to be the little bear's porridge in the story of Goldilocks, not too hot and not too cold, but 'just right'. Putting it simply, it seems from the way the universe is that the universe was meant for the emergence of life, so that the inference to God as the designer who meant or intended this is extremely strong. Even so, there may be other observations that challenge the inference. The point is that the two types of argument (the logical and the inferential) are distinct and do not depend upon each other.

Both, however, attend to the observation of the philosopher Wittgenstein (1889–1951), 'Not *how* the world is, but *that* it is, is the mystery.' The so-called laws of nature indicate how the world is. But what imposes that regularity on the universe? What agent or agents bring it about? The philosopher John Foster spoke for many when he wrote that 'we shall be rationally warranted in concluding that it is God—the God of the theistic account—who creates the laws by imposing the regularities on the world as regularities.... There is a strong case for explaining the regularities by appealing to the agency of God.'

This means that there is an answer to the question, Why is there something rather than nothing? To some it seems a silly question: the universe is simply here and that's it. Why ask why? Richard Dawkins, a well-known popularizer of science, stated in relation to evolution and natural selection, that scientists should never ask the question 'Why?' but only the question 'How?'

That is ridiculous. Scientists constantly ask *both* questions, and one of them, Stephen Hawking, opened the Paralympic Games in 2012 with these words: 'Ever since the dawn of civilisation, people have craved an understanding of the underlying order of the world, why it is as it is and why it exists at all.' There is no reason not to ask that question when we ask it of everything else. The sciences move on by continually asking, not only *how* things are, but also *why* things are as they are, or why things happen or appear as they do. There is no reason in science or philosophy or for that matter in common sense to say that we cannot, or should not, ask why there is a universe. As Brian Davies has put it: 'The fact of the matter is that the existence of the universe is puzzling. If we can ask why things within it are there, we can ask why the universe itself is there.' God is the logically rational and the most probable answer to that question. Or to put it the other way round, whatever is the cause of there being a universe is what we call 'God'.

Flew was persuaded by considerations of that kind, and by other arguments addressed to classic claims relating to Transcendence— concerning, for example, whether an omnipotent and omniscient bodiless person is comprehensible (the questions raised earlier). He concluded with a quotation from David Conway claiming that if his reasoning has been sound, 'there are no good philosophical arguments for denying God to be the explanation of the universe and of the form of order it exhibits.'

Philosophy, therefore, can show that there are good reasons to believe in God, but of course not all people accept them. That is not surprising, since God is more than the conclusion to an argument. There are in any case many other reasons why people believe in God, some of which, it is claimed, are extremely bad (or as Freud put it, 'abject'). We have already met the opinion that ideas about God belong to the infancy of the human race when ignorance prevailed. Now we have come of age, as Bonhoeffer put it, we can (so it is argued) leave the mistakes of juvenile ignorance behind.

This means that attempts to understand why people believe in God are often entangled in speculations about why people *began* to believe in God. If we disentangle the two, we can see that there are both good *and* abject reasons why people believe in God. Even then it is important to remember how often we move from abject points of departure to consequences that transcend them. Freud thought that we approach each other in the case of sex with the physical urges of libido, and with abject and neurotic motives in which the ego tries to get its way. But libido encounters a *responsive other* who, in the very nature of his or her response, can enable the transcendence of the basic need, the abject point of departure.

Consequently Freud came to recognize that we need, not only the language of libido, but also the language of *liebe*, of love. Lust *can* lead to love. Similarly, we may begin to believe in God for abject reasons (such as a fear of hell-fire) but then come to discover, in 'an active meeting and a loving embrace', a wholly responsive Other in whom 'perfect love casts out fear'.

So growing up or 'coming-of-age' does not mean destroying or despising the points of our departure, but rather, with insight, making out of them a character and truth that transcend them. The question of why people believe in God cannot be reduced, as many evidently suppose, to the abject reasons that bring at least some to believe in the first place. So why do people believe in God?

Chapter 2
Why believe in God?

Bonhoeffer believed that educated people will no longer believe in God because God as traditionally understood 'no longer has any pragmatic value for the interpretation or comprehension of nature'. Instead of 'death by a thousand qualifications', 'God' disappears like the grin of the Cheshire cat.

And so it should. Those who argue that belief in God is rational and that, for example, God is the most probable explanation of why there is a universe, do not think that they are offering additional information of pragmatic value about nature or about 'how the universe works'. To come to the rational conclusion that God is the most probable reason why there is something rather than nothing is not to seek additional information about the universe. For that we go to science.

This means that 'the god hypothesis' does not arise from or depend on ill-educated ignorance about the details of the universe—about the flatness of the earth or the spontaneity of the generation of flies, to refer back to Bonhoeffer's examples. The 'god hypothesis' does not tell us 'how the world goes', as Galileo put it long ago. Galileo maintained a principle that he claimed a Cardinal, Cesare Baronio, had taught him: 'The purpose of the Holy Spirit is to teach us how to go to heaven, and not how heaven goes.'

Bonhoeffer was, of course, correct in saying that ideas about God or characterizations of God have been used to offer consolation to people in distress, as also they have been used by politicians to control the people they are governing. For Polybius (2nd century BCE), it explained why the Roman State was so powerful and successful: it clothed in splendid ceremony and ritual what others regard as ignorant superstition:

> They did this, in my view, for the sake of the people. It would have been unnecessary to do so if the State had been composed of wise men, but the people in general are always unstable: they are full of desires outside the law, irrational passion and violent anger. So the people in general must be restrained by hidden terrors and theatrical displays of that kind. Therefore it seems to me that our ancestors were not acting foolishly or without thought in disseminating ideas about the gods together with beliefs in the terrors of Hades, but rather that the people of today are irrational in throwing these things out.

On the other side of the world and at much the same time the Legalists (*fa jia*, the School of Law) in China rejected the Confucian belief that people can be educated into goodness. They held instead that human beings are so naturally inclined to evil that they must be held in place by strong laws with punitive sanctions derived from Tian (usually translated as Heaven), the equivalent in popular belief of God. It was the Legalists who helped Qin Shihuangdi (the first Emperor of the Qin Dynasty, 221–206 BCE) to unify the whole of China for the first time.

Bonhoeffer was also correct in saying that in the past 'God' was brought in to explain why and how things happen. Beliefs about God, in other words, were brought into the gaps of our ignorance in order to provide explanations, and that is 'the God of the gaps' who disappears like the grin of the Cheshire cat as the gaps are filled in.

Change and reliability in understanding God and the universe

What, however, Bonhoeffer missed is the obvious point that just as the sciences correct and change their understandings of the shape and position of the earth (no longer flat and no longer the centre of the universe), and as indeed we correct and change our understandings in general, so also we correct and change our understandings and characterizations of God (no longer with a white beard sitting on a throne just above the clouds).

The changes and corrections are inevitable because, as we have seen, God is not an object among objects in the universe open to direct observation and description. Even if, as Aquinas maintained, it is possible to demonstrate logically and rationally that God is, it will still be the case that, while the words or pictures into which beliefs about God are put serve many purposes not least of prayer and worship, they are always inadequate (as those who pray know better than most) and are necessarily open to correction and change.

A consequence of this is that there is not a single and agreed 'God-hypothesis', to use Bonhoeffer's term. There are many hypotheses about God and many different characterizations of God in the different religions, even among those that are based on what is believed to be Revelation—as, for example, in the Bible, Quran, or Veda. As we will see, the characterization of God in the Quran for Muslims is very different from the characterization of God in the Vedas in India.

That happens because even if the words of Revelation are regarded by believers as the literal 'Word of God', the actual words are expressed in particular languages at particular times. In contrast to *God*, they are embedded in contingent and changing circumstances which affect what can be said or written at any particular time. As a result, no claimed Revelation contains a single 'God-hypothesis', but contains, rather, change and variety in what is believed about God.

Thus, to give an example, in India the supreme and ultimate Reality is Brahman. Can we give any description of what Brahman is like? In the Upanishads (part of Indian Scripture), some texts say that Brahman is utterly Transcendent and cannot be described, but other texts describe Brahman vividly. Since, as Chari puts it, 'Śruti [Scripture] is the final authority in spiritual matters,...how are we to overcome such a conflict?' Some interpreted the texts to claim that the conflict can be explained away, but others recognized the conflict and said that earlier texts describing Brahman have been superseded by the later in a process of displacement known as *apacchedanyaya* (literally, letting go of someone in a ritual procession).

A comparable process occurs even in the Quran. Muslims believe that the Quran is God's Word 'given' (Arabic *waha*') or 'sent down' (*nazala*, hence *tanzil*, the common word for 'revelation') to Muhammad during a period so short (roughly 20 years) that there might not seem any opportunity or even reason for correction and change. Yet Muslims themselves recognize that in the Quran early 'revelations' are (to use the technical word) 'abrogated' by later ones in relation to the changing circumstances and experiences of Muhammad's life.

It is of course claimed by many that the words of Revelation reveal God with such complete certainty that they are in effect God, and scrolls or texts containing what is believed to be Revelation are often treated with extreme reverence. It is clearly true that they express the *consequence* of God in and through different people and different languages in their extremely different contingent circumstances, and it is equally true that those words continue to mediate God into many human lives with immense authority. But those differences mean that the limitations (and opportunities) of contingency remain.

It follows that Revelation has to be *interpreted*, and rival interpretations can lead to change, disagreement and even conflict in what is believed about the nature and character of God. Religions have very different understandings of how that work of interpretation should be undertaken. The fact, nevertheless, remains that words have to be interpreted, and as a result characterizations and beliefs about God change and are different, not just between religions, but also within a religion.

So even in the context of Revelation, the words and pictures that are used about God are always and necessarily provisional and inadequate, and are thus open to correction and change. But that is true of much more than the words we use about God. It is true also of the sciences *even though* the universe is available for observation in a way that God is not. The equations of science, the basic mathematical rules that govern the universe, map the laws of physics. But the observations and the inferences that are drawn are not exhaustively conclusive, and no scientist can tell us finally and completely 'what the universe is'.

Although, therefore, the claims of science are advanced rightly with great confidence, and although it is often taken for granted that the claims of science are 'absolutely true and completely certain', yet in fact there is much about them that is approximate, provisional, corrigible (open to correction), and even wrong from a later point of view. That is why Richard Feynman, who shared the Nobel Prize for physics in 1965, started his introductory lectures on physics by emphasizing, as Isaac Newton did before him, that there is in science 'an expanding frontier of ignorance':

> Each piece, or part, of the whole of nature is always merely an *approximation* to the complete truth, or the complete truth so far as we know it. In fact, everything we know is only some kind of approximation, because *we know that we do not know all the laws* as yet. Therefore, things must be learned only to be unlearned again or, more likely, to be corrected.

So the claims of science are corrigible and incomplete, and may even be wrong from a later point of view. But they can, nevertheless, be extremely accurate and reliable because they are, so to speak, wrong about *something*: the universe is (so far) consistently what it is, even though we can only speak of it corrigibly.

So too with accounts of God. No one can tell us finally and completely 'what God is like'. Accounts of God, even those derived from what is believed to be Revelation, are approximate, corrigible and incomplete. But they can nevertheless be reliable because they are wrong about some One with whom, as we will see, interaction is possible. So when people try to say something about God, it is inevitable that they use words and pictures that are extremely approximate and corrigible. It is, however, very important to remember that the signpost is not the same as that to which it points. The issue is whether the language, however inadequate, points the way to something that is truly the case, and exactly the same consideration applies to the language and models of science.

Clearly there is then an immense difference between claims about God and claims about the universe, since God is not an object in the universe and is therefore not available for inspection in a scientific way. So the questions then immediately arise: in what ways is that interaction with God possible? How have humans come to realize that their belief in God is reliable no matter how often the pictures and words have to be changed through which they have tried to say something about God? How has it come about that beliefs about God, however much they may differ from each other, are so widespread that for most of human history they have been universal? Why do people believe in God?

Many different answers have been given to those questions. Some come from behavioural sciences like 'sociology, anthropology, and psychology' (the subtitle of my book *The Sense of God*). Others come from the part that beliefs in God play in history, politics, and economics. Others come from aesthetics and from the part that beliefs in God play in imagination and in the sense of inspiration.

It is not possible in a Short Introduction to summarize these, but some have already appeared. Thus two of them are in Bonhoeffer's list of reasons why, in his view, belief in God will survive 'in the shelter of lazy minds': that of Marx (belief in God is a powerful weapon in the hands of vested interests to maintain the exploitation of the workers); and that of Freud (belief in God is an illusion that only the psychopathologically disabled and the lazy-minded will 'buy into' because they cannot face reality and need compensation in the next life for the miseries of this).

Those are examples of functional explanations: they observe what functions beliefs in God have served, and they conclude that that is how and why those beliefs began. Other explanations are more structural, focusing, for example, on the structures of the human body and brain, and on what they enable people to experience and feel. An early speculation suggested that the power of an emotion like anger, fear or lust is sometimes so *overwhelmingly* strong that it feels as though an external and personal agent is responsible for them.

Neuroscience and experience

In recent years many different explanations have drawn on the rapid expansion of brain research, and these have had important implications for claims to the experience of God and for religious experience in general. For example, the exploration during the 20th century of the functions and interactions of the two hemispheres of the brain led to the theory of Julian Jaynes, who located 'the origin of consciousness in the bicameral mind' (to quote the title of his book), resulting, in his view, in one hemisphere receiving inputs from the other and interpreting them as the 'voice of God'.

Another early example linked brain research to genetics and produced what is known as 'biogenetic structuralism'. This explored how the genes and proteins programme and build the structures of the brain (and body) in such a way that they prepare us for characteristic behaviours. They prepare us, for example, for the ability to breathe, to speak languages, to engage in sex, to find and eat food, and so on. They do not *determine* what in detail we will say or eat, or how exactly we will behave sexually, but they *prepare* us to be human in those fundamental ways. They also prepare us for the recognition of God. The warning, 'Prepare to meet thy God' has been transformed into the observation, 'Prepared to meet thy God'.

A book summarizing that work, *Why God Won't Go Away*, ends with the claim that 'the neurobiological roots of spiritual transcendence' lead people into a sense of union with that which is completely real and absolute far beyond the limits of material existence:

> As long as our brains are arranged the way they are, as long as our minds are capable of sensing this deeper reality, spirituality will continue to shape the human experience, and God, however we define that majestic, mysterious concept, will not go away.

We are prepared, therefore, in the brain for experiences of an unforgettable kind. But what experiences? There is a helpful survey and review of these in a book by David Hay which concludes that 'spiritual awareness is a necessary part of our biology, whatever our religious beliefs or lack of them.' At one extreme, human emotions lead many to a passionate participation in the reality of God. Spinoza was called by Novalis 'a God-intoxicated man', but he is only one among many. At another extreme is the experience of AUB—Absolute Unitary Being. This is a surprisingly common experience in which the difference between one's self and the universe is obliterated: there is no sense of the passing of time, and all that remains is a perfect, timeless, undifferentiated consciousness—often described as a state of bliss. Not surprisingly many have felt that in this experience they have 'met God'.

There are, of course, others who have found that experience equally certain and memorable, but who have not concluded that it was an experience of *God*. Bertrand Russell was once possessed by 'a sort of mystic illumination' and as a result he 'became a completely different person', but he went on to write *Why I Am Not a Christian*; Kenneth Clark 'was radiated by a kind of heavenly joy' which made him sure that he had 'felt the finger of God', but he walked away from the experience because he knew that otherwise he would have to reform his life. Claims about God based on experience are, as we have seen, inferences that are drawn abductively from what we experience, but it must, therefore, be the case that some refuse or prefer not to draw the inference of God.

That, however, does not invalidate the often amazing consequence for those who do. The multitude of ways in which humans have experienced the world, their relations with each other, and their own personal lives have evoked the belief that it is God who brings those experiences into being, who sustains them and is at work in and through them—and that it is God who, in some instances, is encountered in them.

So the drama, beauty and mysterious otherness of the world can create a strong sense of awe and wonder—and fear. Rudolph Otto (1869–1937) called this the sense of 'the numinous' (Latin *numen*, roughly 'Divinity'). 'The idea of the holy' (to quote the English title of his book *Das Heilige*, 1917) creates a fundamental and basic way in which humans experience the world as utterly different from themselves, inviting or enticing, but also terrifying. It is, to use his words, *mysterium tremendum fascinans* [or *fascinosum*] *et augustum*, the experience of whatever inspires both dread and fascination beyond rational analysis. Applied to God, it is, to quote

Hepburn's paraphrase, 'the distinctive experience of God, at once inevitably transcendent, remote, yet stirring a recognition that here is the primary source of beauty and love.'

None of that is uncommon, and it has reinforced the way in which the vast majority of people throughout human history have lived their lives with an awareness of God—lives in which God, however understood or characterized, is at the very least a background assumption or 'an embedded belief'. God is then experienced as one who is active in many ways, and as one with whom (in equally many different ways) people can interact—in, for example, prayer, worship and ritual. In other words, they live their lives with God extremely close at hand. As the Quran puts it (50.16), 'It was we who created Man, and we know what whispers within him, for we are closer to him than the vein in his neck.' They live in the presence of God and as a consequence of God—but of God imagined or understood in vastly different ways.

That immense variety is hardly surprising given that God is not an object among objects that can be observed and described. Philosophers and theologians are right that if God is, then it is *God* that God must be, eternal and unchanging. But that does not alter the fact that in human history words, beliefs and ideas about God are constantly challenged and changed.

That is inevitable and necessary because religions are set in worlds which are themselves constantly changing and which therefore offer both challenge and opportunity to give new expression to practices and beliefs. John Henry Newman (1801–91, a Christian theologian and philosopher) emphasized the point: belief develops in what he called 'the busy scene of human life' by engaging with it and by 'entering into strange territory' where changes are unceasing: 'It [belief] changes with them in order to remain the same. In a higher world it is otherwise, but here below to live is to change, and to be perfect is to have changed often.'

It certainly does not follow that all proposed or actual change is for the better or that it automatically equals progress. That is clearly false. But it is equally false to conclude that no change is ever necessary or desirable. Sometimes, of course, it may not be necessary, as, for example, in small-scale religions in stable environments. But in Newman's 'busy scene of human life', he was right to insist that change is necessary for the sake of truth.

By no means all believers accept that. Indeed, many insist that the world ('the busy scene of human life') must never set the agenda for religion. But in fact the world always and rightly 'sets the agenda', not just for religion but even for God, since otherwise God would not, for example, become incarnate or reveal a word of truth to address or rescue people who are in particular and specific circumstances of need.

Nevertheless, nostalgia for the past occurs in all religions, a longing, perhaps, for a Golden Age (of the Apostles, for example, or of the al-Rashidun, the first four Caliphs) when, so it is claimed, belief was pure and uncorrupted: the way forward has to be the way back to the golden past. People can live successfully in that way, as Jung observed, but the consequence is increasing schism in human community:

> There are people who, psychologically, might just as well have lived in the year 5,000 B.C., i.e., who can still successfully solve their conflicts as people did 7,000 years ago. There are countless barbarians and men of antiquity in Europe…, and a great number of mediaeval Christians. On the other hand, there are relatively few who have reached the degree of consciousness possible in our time.

As in the sciences so here: there is much from the past to be conserved, but there is equally much that has to be, and constantly is, changed and corrected. If change is resisted, it can result in those characterizations of God that Dawkins singled out specifically to attack in *The God Delusion*—an attack with which many believers in God would sympathize. Through history many understandings and characterizations of God have been questioned and corrected while at the same time many others have been secured and confirmed. *Both* processes have been decisive in creating and transforming the human understanding of God.

The tensions in that process have led to conflicts and even wars of religion, but they have led also to learning, assimilation and sharing: Aquinas combined Aristotle with the Christian tradition and produced what came to be known as Thomism. Udayana combined Nyaya and Vaisheshika in a way that led to Navya-nyaya, New Logic.

A Short Introduction cannot summarize the whole 'history of God', but by taking examples from well-known religious traditions, we can begin to see how the process of *conservation yet also of change* works out in practice. Even in the examples chosen only some key moments can be explored. Thus the next chapter begins with Judaism and the foundations in the Biblical period in order to show how the distinctive Jewish understandings of God came to be established, and how also those early characterizations of God were already beginning to be changed and developed within the Biblical period itself. On those foundations were built the further and dazzling developments of the rabbis, of Kabbalah, of Maimonides, of the Hasidim, and of liturgy and prayer, to mention only the most obvious, but none of that can be understood unless we understand first what the foundations are. 'In the beginning God...', as the Jewish Bible begins. And it is to those beginnings that we now turn.

Chapter 3

The religions of Abraham: Jewish understandings of God

So far we have begun to see why the words and pictures we use of God are bound to be provisional and corrigible (open to correction), and we have recognized that the same is true of the words and pictures of the sciences in relation to their own subject-matter. The sciences achieve and conserve immense reliability but they are always open to change and correction. In a comparable way, ideas and beliefs about God have achieved and conserved their own kind of reliability while at the same time constantly needing to be changed and corrected in particular ways. In the case of God, the process of correction and change is entirely different from that of the sciences, but it does nevertheless occur and it is often a matter, not of calm debate, but of fierce contest and conflict, as for example, in the Reformations of Western Christianity in Europe.

The process of conservation and change can be seen with particular clarity throughout the roughly 3,000 years during which the religions known now as Judaism, Christianity, and Islam came into being. Those religions are known as 'the Abrahamic religions' because they are related to each other by their recognition of Abraham (in Islam and Arabic, Ibrahim) as their common ancestor (*Genesis* 12.1; *Galatians* 3.7; *Quran* 2.130/6). Each of those religions changed radically the existing characterizations of God, and yet it also conserved and continued what came before it.

The process of challenge and change is even true of the very beginning (historically) of the process that led to the Jewish understanding of God. That understanding is rooted in the writings that make up the Jewish Bible (Greek *biblia*, 'Books'), a collection of many works of different kinds written over a period of roughly 1,500 years. It is known by Jews as Miqra ('reading' or recital), HaSefarim (The Books), or, in an acronym made up of its three component parts, as Tanach (Torah, the first five books, Nebiim, the Prophets, and Ketubim, the Writings). The name Torah is also (and often) used of the whole of Jewish Scripture.

Overall, Tanach tells the story of how a group of nomadic herdsmen (*Deuteronomy* 26.5) came to believe that God has called them to specific work and responsibilities in the world. But it tells the story, not as a Greek historian like Thucydides might have told it, but with the sense that the author of the story is God, from whom the world, the events of history, and even the words themselves of the story ultimately come. That sense of God taking the initiative to inspire people to live, speak, and write in 'the path of life' that God desires (*Psalm* 16.11) led eventually to particular words being gathered into the collection known as Tanach. The words in Tanach have authority because they are believed to come from God as the author of all things in creation.

The Canaanites and the Promised Land

The process was a long one through which the people eventually known as the Jews came to their understanding of God. It involved change and correction, not least of existing beliefs. A dramatic moment came when, according to the biblical account, Abraham was told by God to 'arise and go' (*Genesis* 12.1) from his home in Mesopotamia to a new land that God promised to give him so that he could become the founding father of a great nation.

In that promise of the Land lie the seeds of conflict that continue to the present-day: for whose land was it—and is it now? In the days of Abraham, 'the promised land' was already inhabited by a number of different peoples including the Canaanites and the Amorites. The Canaanites lived mainly on the east Mediterranean coast (their name, like that of the Amorites, may mean 'those who live where the sun goes down'), but they also moved inland to an area covering what is now Israel/Palestine. The Canaanites were skilful and creative people. They even invented, much to our benefit, a form of writing much simpler than the cumbersome cuneiform of Mesopotamia or the hieroglyphics of Egypt: they invented the alphabet. No longer reliant on oral transmission, that invention made possible the *writing down* of the words that ended up in Tanach—in which, ironically, the descendants of Abraham recorded God's command to them to destroy the Canaanites.

The problem was that the Canaanites were inhabiting the land that was now believed to have been promised to Abraham and his descendants. The descendants of Abraham were originally a group of related families (or 'tribes') known as the Bene Jacob ('sons of Jacob', who was the grandson of Abraham) or (Jacob's other name) Bene Israel—hence Israelites, the forerunners of the Jews. They were told that they can only possess the Promised Land if they utterly destroy its inhabitants including the Canaanites:

> As for the towns of these peoples that the Lord your God is giving you as an inheritance, you must not let anything that breathes remain alive. You shall annihilate them—the Hittites and the Amorites, the Canaanites and the Perizzites, the Hivites and the Jebusites—just as the Lord your God has commanded, so that they may not teach you to do all the forbidden things that they do for their gods, and you thus sin against the Lord your God.

That is a dramatic illustration of how radical the changes in the understanding and characterization of God can be. The people are commanded, not just to drive out Canaanites and others, but also to reject their beliefs about God—'the forbidden things that they do for their gods'. Even so, they absorbed some of those beliefs, not least the names of God. The Canaanites believed in a supreme God known as El who appoints agents (*elohim*, 'gods') to run the world for him, and they in turn appoint supervisors, Baalim ('lords' or 'owners'), who look after the land and ensure its fertility for those who pay them the right sort of attention in ritual and sacrifice.

Those were the gods whose worship the Israelites were told to shun. Many of them were not too keen to do so. When they began to take over 'the Promised Land' (i.e., Canaanite territory), they actually absorbed a great deal of Canaanite belief and culture, not least its system of writing that made Tanach possible. In general, many of them were happy to seek prosperity and fertility and anything else on offer from the Baalim, the owners of the land; and they were equally happy to acknowledge El (also called Baal in the singular) as the supreme God who, by overcoming chaos, had created a world of order—traces of those early creation stories can still be found in Jewish Scripture (e.g., *Psalm* 74.12–7; 89.9–13).

That easy-going relationship with the Canaanites and their gods changed completely as a result of the great escape from Egypt known as 'the Exodus'. During a period of famine, families of the kinship group, the Bene Jacob, moved to Egypt in search of food. They were subordinated there as slaves. They escaped under the leadership of Moses who believed that he was commanded and enabled to do this by God—but God with a name and character that they had not previously known.

What was that name? YHWH. That may look baffling, but because Hebrew words are written without the vowels being included, we do not know how that name was pronounced. Conventionally it is now pronounced Yahweh, but those vowels are a guess. Jews believe that just as God is holy (utterly different and far removed from everything that corrupts and contaminates), so also this name is holy—so holy, in fact, that many Jews make no attempt to pronounce it and prefer to say instead HaShem, 'the Name'. In the Hebrew Bible they put into the four letters YHWH the vowels taken from the word Adonai which means 'my Lord'. That explains why in many English translations YHWH appears as 'the Lord' (with El/Elohim translated as 'God'), and it explains also how the earliest English translations arrived at the impossible name Jehovah by trying to read YHWH with the vowels taken from Adonai.

The book in the Bible called (from its first word) *Shemoth*, or in English *Exodus*, tells how, under the guidance of Yahweh (a pillar of cloud by day and of fire by night), Moses led the people through the wilderness and received from Yahweh the instructions and laws (including the Ten Commandments) which the people must obey if God is to continue to protect and help them. This is the foundation of Torah (see Figure 2).

When those who had escaped from Egypt arrived back in the Promised Land, they formed a union, which was sealed in a new agreement, or Covenant, based on the recognition that 'Yahweh is the El of Israel' (*Joshua* 24.2). The Covenant required, according to *Joshua*, a complete rejection of all other gods, including those that they and their ancestors had served, and a total commitment to Yahweh:

> Now therefore revere Yahweh, and serve him in sincerity and in faithfulness; put away the gods that your ancestors served beyond the River [in Mesopotamia] and in Egypt, and serve Yahweh. Now if you are unwilling to serve Yahweh, choose this day whom you will serve, whether the gods your ancestors served in the region beyond the River or the gods of the Amorites in whose land you are living; but as for me and my house, we will serve Yahweh.

Here the conflict between different characterizations of God becomes inevitable, and Tanach is organized to tell the story of

2. A scroll of Torah (end of Numbers and beginning of Deuteronomy) is held up before the western retaining wall of the Temple Mount in Jerusalem. A focus of prayer for Jews, the Western Wall was called The Wailing Wall by people who saw Jews mourning the destruction of the Second Temple

how Yahweh takes over what El ('God') was believed by the Canaanites to be and to do until eventually El simply becomes another name for Yahweh ('the Lord'). As for the Baalim, they are challenged, and derided as false gods who cannot do what they are supposed to do.

That challenge was led particularly by the prophets of Yahweh. They were people who felt themselves to be in-breathed or inspired by God to speak the word of God to kings and commoners alike: their messages of judgement, encouragement and interpretation of events often begin, 'Thus says the Lord [Yahweh]'. To one of them, Jeremiah (6th century), the urgency of this in-breathing felt like a fire burning in his bones that he could not resist (*Jeremiah* 20.9).

The directness of the prophetic challenge can be seen in the dramatic story told of the prophet, Elijah, who entered into a contest with the prophets of the Baals to make the people see that Yahweh is the only true God. Elijah and the 450 prophets of Baal prepare sacrifices of a bull to see which of the two, Yahweh or Baal, will bring fire to consume the offering. Baal fails to do so, but then Elijah prays to 'Yahweh, the Elohim of Abraham, Isaac, and Israel' to show that Yahweh alone is truly God:

> Then the fire of Yahweh fell and consumed the burnt offering.... When all the people saw it, they fell on their faces and said, 'Yahweh indeed is God [Elohim]; Yahweh indeed is God.' Elijah said to them, 'Seize the prophets of Baal; do not let one of them escape.' Then they seized them; and Elijah brought them down to the Wadi Kishon, and killed them there.

David, the Temple, and the Messiah

A less dramatic but equally momentous and long-lasting change in the characterization of God occurred when (from *c.*1150–1000 BCE) the Philistines (seafaring marauders from Greece), who had settled on the Mediterranean coast, began to move inland. To meet the threat David called together and tried to unite the families of the kinship group, the Bene Jacob, who had been living largely independent lives. He captured Jerusalem from the Jebusites and made it a neutral capital for the new coalition. He also took from the Jebusites the idea of having a central shrine to draw people together in the worship of Yahweh. He brought to Jerusalem the Ark, the focal symbol of God's presence during the wanderings in the Wilderness, but it was left to his son, Solomon, to build the First Temple. The Second Temple was built after the Exile (see Figure 3).

This was a radical change in the understanding of God, and it met with angry resistance among the tradition-conservatives who said that Yahweh had never lived in a house, had no need of a house, and had looked after the people perfectly well in the Wilderness by moving around with them. Despite the opposition, the Temple was built. There priests performed the rituals and sacrifices of praise and penitence, and prophets in their day saw visions of God: 'In the year that King Uzziah died [c.738 BCE], I saw the Lord sitting on a throne, high and lofty; and the hem of his robe filled the Temple.'

The Temple became for the Jews the most sacred place on earth. At its heart was was the Holy of Holies, a small, empty room with no windows which only the High Priest was allowed to enter, and even he could only do this on the Day of Atonement, Yom Kippur, the day when sins are forgiven and people are made once more at one with God: 'He shall make atonement…because of the uncleannesses of the people of Israel, and because of their transgressions, all their sins.'

David introduced another change that had equally long-lasting consequences. Again from the Jebusites he took the idea of the king providing the bridge between God and the people. Solemnly anointed, the king became the conduit through whom the

God

3. A large-scale model in Jerusalem shows the Second Temple with the surrounding Court of the Gentiles. In the centre are the Court of Women, the Court of Israel (for men), and the Court of Priests (not visible). The Holy of Holies is within the central Shrine

blessings of God would flow to the people. 'The anointed one' is in Hebrew *hamashiach*, which has come into English as 'the messiah'. So began the belief that messiahs (kings and high priests) are the specially appointed agents of God on earth. When most of the actual kings (the actual messiahs) failed, the hopes invested in God's Anointed were not abandoned: they were transferred into the future in the belief that God will send a Messiah one day to establish God's rule (or kingdom) on earth. The building of the Temple and the belief in the Messiah completely changed the understanding of God and of God's relation to the people.

Suffering and death

Many other changes and corrections were made during the course of Biblical history. For example, there is in Tanach hardly any belief that there will be a worthwhile afterlife beyond death. Yes, there might be a memory of the dead in Sheol, the darkness of the grave, but certainly nothing to look forward to and definitely no compensation for the pains and inequalities of this world—the complete opposite of what Freud and many others have assumed about the origin of religious belief. This means that all the astonishing words in Tanach celebrating the way in which God cares for Israel (as, for example, a mother cares for a child, *Isaiah* 66.13) came into being without any belief that this faithful care would continue after death. Only at the very end of the Biblical period did they begin to realize that the faithfulness of God during this life might continue after death.

Equally dramatic was the gradual change in beliefs about suffering. It was originally believed (and appears widely in Tanach) that if people suffer, it must be because they have done wrong (i.e., have sinned) and are being punished by God. Since wrong-doers often 'spring up like grass' and 'flourish like a bay tree' (*Psalms* 92.7, 37.35), whereas the sinless like Job (in the book of that name, which rejects the older understanding) suffer greatly, the old view that 'where you see suffering there you see sin' was contradicted and displaced. Thus when in the 6th century BCE the Babylonians destroyed Jerusalem and took its people into captivity (the Exile), the sufferings of the people were interpreted in *Isaiah* 53 as those of a faithful Suffering Servant (Israel) who is being punished for the sins of *others*—an understanding of suffering and death later applied by Christians to the crucifixion.

What is remarkable about Tanach is that the early characterizations of God are preserved: they are not cut out or erased. It is like the way in which parents keep the earliest attempts of their children to write or draw: they are childish and immature, but they are very precious. It is God who 'is the One that is' ('I Am who I Am' is a possible meaning of the name YHWH) and who is consistently and enduringly the same from one age to another: it is their own understanding which has to change and grow.

Tanach, therefore, retains in its text the early words and beliefs that have been developed much further, but even so they were still regarded as words derived from God. Tanach is thus a record of the long process through which the understanding and the characterization of God develop and change, as the people through successive generations come to know more wisely the name and nature of the One who has called them into being and with whom they have to deal. Indeed, they came to identify Wisdom itself as the agent of God in creation and in their own lives. When that profound affirmation of Wisdom was combined with Greek philosophy and science it produced the scientific revolutions of the Western world.

One God and holiness

In the end the single greatest consequence of that long process of change and correction was a recognition that if what is thought to be God turns out truly to be *God*, it is God that God turns out to be. It sounds complicated, but it is extremely simple. In the midst of all the many different beliefs and characterizations of God and Goddess in the world in which they lived (Melkart, Milkom, Tammuz, Dagon, Asherah, Anat, Astarte, to mention only a few), they came to the realization that there can only be whatever God is. There cannot be many gods or bits of God in competition with each other, one god for the Canaanites, another for the Jews. There can only be the One who is God, the creator of all things and of all people.

It led to the single most important command to the Jewish people: Hear! Listen! *Shema*! The command known as the Shema ('hear') is the foundation stone of the Jewish understanding of God which adult Jewish men are required to recite twice daily: *shema Israel: Adonai Eloheynu Adonai ehad*; Hear, Israel; YHWH our God YHWH One, i.e., 'The Lord is our God, the Lord is One', or 'The Lord our God is the Lord alone', and other slight variants in translation that arise because the word 'is' does not appear in the Hebrew. Whatever the exact meaning, the affirmation is clear: in the case of God there is nothing other than God—the foundation of what is known as 'monotheism', or in Hebrew *yihud haShem*, the unity of God. As Maimonides (1135–1204), the great Jewish philosopher and systematizer of Law, put it:

> God is One. He is neither one of two nor more than two, but One. There are things existing in the universe to which the term 'one' is applied, but it is nothing like the Oneness of God. It is not one among many, nor one body made up of many parts. There is no singularity in the world that resembles the Oneness of God.

The Jewish people, therefore, are bound together in an agreement or Covenant with God which is derived, in their belief, from the initiative of God in creating and giving order to all things, and in calling this particular or chosen people to demonstrate on behalf of the whole world what it means to live 'under the eye and by the strength of God'.

To be in that close bond with God, 'the high and lofty One who inhabits eternity, whose name is Holy' (*Isaiah* 57.15), the people must live in that same condition of holiness. The terms and conditions of the Covenant tell them how that can be done, and how therefore they can obey the command that constitutes Israel: 'You shall be holy, for I the Lord your God am holy' (*Leviticus* 19.2). That is why, for example, it is a characterizing mark of the Jews as the Covenant people that they 'keep the Sabbath day holy' in imitation of God who rested on the seventh day of Creation (*Exodus* 20.8–11).

It follows that there is a right way to live and that people can know what it is. As one of the Prophets put it briefly (*Micah* 6.8): 'God has told you what is good: and what does the Lord require of you but to do justice, and love kindness, and to walk humbly with your God?' If the people 'walk' according to the terms and conditions of the Covenant, they receive the protection, guidance, and blessing of God; otherwise they are punished, not least by other nations whom God brings against them like a plague of flies and a swarm of stinging bees (*Isaiah* 7.18). This is fundamental in the Jewish understanding of God, as it is summarized, for example, in *Deuteronomy*:

> Know therefore that the Lord [Yahweh] your God [Elohim] is God [El], the faithful God who maintains covenant loyalty with those who love him and keep his commandments, to a thousand generations, and who repays in their own person those who reject him. He does not delay but repays in their own person those who reject him. Therefore, observe diligently the commandment—the statutes and the ordinances—that I am commanding you today....

When Jews undertake that obedience, they do so, not just for their own sake, but for the sake of the whole world so that all people can see what it means in practice to be at one with God.

> Thus says the Lord of Hosts: In those days [in the future when God's rule is established] ten men from nations of every language

shall take hold of a Jew, grasping his garment and saying, 'Let us go with you, for we have heard that God is with you.' (*Zechariah* 8.23)

It is a vision that God will displace all other false gods and idols and will create through this chosen people a new world:

Thus says God [El], the Lord [Yahweh], who created the heavens and stretched them out, who spread out the earth and what comes from it, who gives breath to the people upon it and spirit to those who walk in it:

I am the Lord, I have called you in righteousness, I have taken you by the hand and kept you; I have given you as a covenant to the people, a light to the nations, to open the eyes that are blind, to bring out the prisoners from the dungeon, from the prison those who sit in darkness.

I am the Lord, that is my name; my glory I give to no other, nor my praise to idols.

See, the former things have come to pass, and new things I now declare; before they spring forth, I tell you of them.

It is an awesome obligation, particularly when Jews have tried to keep faith and yet have suffered endless persecutions culminating in the Holocaust (*haShoah*, 'the disaster'). Where, in the disaster, was the God of the Covenant promises? For some it was a test of faith to the extreme limit evoking an 11th Commandment, 'Thou shalt survive'. For others it was beyond explanation:

Solly Gitnick said a prayer
Standing on the washroom stair:
'Lord, we are your chosen race;
For Christ's sake choose another, in our place.'
God did so. Or so some others thought.
In God's name, they pursued and caught
Young Solly Gitnick in his prayer,
And killed him on the washroom stair.

That poem, 'Anti-Semitism', is pointing to another radical change in the understanding and characterization of God—though the phrase 'radical change' is surely too mild to describe what Runes has called 'the war against the Jew':

> No group or nation or alliance of nations in all known history has ever perpetrated on a hapless minority such sadistic atrocities over so long a time as the Christians have on the Jews. Not one denomination or another, but *all* did, and especially those of the Catholic faith.

The pogroms to which he refers were undertaken by those who believed that this was what God wanted them to do. It was, to say the least, a disjunctive change in the understanding and characterization of God.

God

Chapter 4

The religions of Abraham: Christian understandings of God

The participation of Christians in anti-Semitism and the persecution of Jews is all the more tragically terrible because the earliest 'Christians' were for the most part Jews. They were, however, Jews who believed that a man from Galilee called Jesus was the promised Messiah (for the Jewish understanding of Messiah, see Chapter 3). The Greek word for *hamashiach* ('the anointed one') is in Greek *ho Christos*, hence Jesus Christ. Those believers were not called 'Christians' until some years after his death (*Acts* 11.26).

This means that the movement now known as Christianity began as one interpretation among many at that time of what it should mean to live in the Covenant relationship with God. Jews shared in common the belief that they were called by God to live as the Covenant people, and they knew that the basic terms and conditions of that agreement were contained in Torah. But how are the commands and prohibitions to be observed in a world that is constantly changing? Life in Jerusalem under the Romans was entirely different from life in the Sinai desert, and sacrifice under the stars was very different from the ritual and liturgy of the Temple. What does God want now?

The Covenant and Torah

In the 1st century CE (when Jesus was alive), there were many
different answers to that question. Some thought that they should
stick as closely as possible to the texts and traditions from the past
(the final list of the Books, HaSefarim, making up the Bible, was
not decided for another 200 years, but most of them were already
recognized as having God-derived authority). Among the
text-conservatives were the Sadducees, the priests and their
associates in the Temple, who kept as closely as they could to what
God had commanded. They could not, for example, accept the
speculation that there will be a life after death because it is not in
the books of Moses (Torah).

Others did not deny the authority of the texts, but believed that
the commands and prohibitions must be able to be applied to
new and changed circumstances. The Temple in Jerusalem, for
example, remained the centre of the world (maps as late as the
Middle Ages placed it there), but Jews were now dispersed
throughout the Mediterranean world in the Diaspora (Greek,
'dispersion'). What became known as Rabbinic Judaism worked
out how the terms of the Covenant could still be kept even at the
far end of the Mediterranean—and now around the world. For
example, they created 'places of assembly', or Synagogues, as local
centres running in parallel with the Temple and with equivalent
practices—all the more important after the destruction of
Jerusalem in 135 CE.

To enable people to keep the terms and conditions of the
Covenant, they developed ways of interpreting Torah to make it
'liveable' so that the foundation command (*Leviticus* 19.2), 'You
shall be holy, for I the Lord your God am holy', can be obeyed by
all, wherever they live, and not just by an elite in the protected
geography of the Temple. For example, the brief command to keep
the Sabbath day holy produced so many questions (e.g., does

pressing a button in an elevator/lift on the Sabbath count as work or not?) and so many answers that the interpretations were called 'a mountain hanging by a hair'.

The 'interpreters' were known as exactly that, *perushim*, or in its English form, Pharisees, who became known eventually as the Rabbis. Their purpose was to help people to live in the Covenant with God in contrast to the literalists (like the Sadducees) who insisted on the detail of the Law as originally revealed. Among the interpreters there were two extremes. The majority looked for interpretations that would *help* people to live in a covenant relationship with God. Others insisted that since the laws have now been interpreted to apply to new circumstances, they must be obeyed: there is no excuse not to do so (those are the Pharisees attacked as rigorists in the Gospels). That division continues to the present-day between the ultra-Orthodox Jews (such as the Haredim insisting on the detail of the Law) and the Reform or Liberal Jews: it results in different understandings of 'what God wants'.

When Jesus was alive, the disputes were at their height about what it should mean in practice to live as the Covenant people. He taught initially in Galilee where there were many synagogues, and it is clear that he sided emphatically with those who wished to make the Covenant with God liveable, and in that way to establish the Kingdom of God on earth. He taught his followers to pray, 'Father, hallowed be your name. Your kingdom come on earth as in heaven.'

But what would the Kingdom be like when it comes? Jesus shared in a general way the Biblical understanding and characterization of God, but he was very independent in his understanding of what the rule or the Kingdom of God on earth means in practice.

Basically, Jesus did not believe that 'doing the will of God on earth' is *only* possible with strict obedience to the detail of the Law. He believed that the Kingdom is open, without any conditions, to all who turn to God in trust and to their neighbour in love. When asked to say which of the many commandments was the most fundamental, he answered by putting two together (*Deuteronomy* 6.5 and *Leviticus* 19.18):

> 'You shall love the Lord your God with all your heart, and with all your soul, and with all your mind.' This is the greatest and first commandment. And a second is like it: 'You shall love your neighbour as yourself.' On these two commandments hang all the law and the prophets.

Jesus taught about the Kingdom of God and what it means (especially through parables), but he also put that meaning into action and life. The Kingdom does not lie only in some distant future: the signs of its reality are already here, and Jesus pointed to the signs of the Kingdom, not just in the way in which he taught its meaning, but also in the way in which he healed people and pronounced that their sins have been forgiven. All this was completely unconditional: it did not depend on keeping the Law, or on having the right ideas about God. For Jesus, openness to God in faith and love is fundamental (and is possible for non-Jews as well as Jews), but even that is not a condition of God's works of healing and forgiveness. In that context, keeping the Law is neither a necessary condition nor a sufficient guarantee of approval in God's sight.

Jesus and God

Jesus saw God challenging and overturning many of the received attitudes (often prejudices) of the world, setting the poor before the rich, sinners before the self-righteous, children before their teachers, the last before the first. He stressed the lengths to which God will go to seek and find the lost, and he warned of the anger of God against those who despise or hurt those, such as children, who are defenceless.

In itself, that might just about be regarded as an interpretation of what it must mean to live in the Covenant relationship with God, even though it did not give priority to keeping the laws that define the Covenant. But what was disturbing and threatening to *other* interpretations was the way in which Jesus acted and taught with a striking independence, which he claimed came to him directly from God. He made real in the world things that it was believed only God can do—the healing of the sick and the forgiveness of sins, combined with unmistakeable authority in his teaching about the meaning and implications of God. Jesus seemed, to many of those who met him, to be expressing the meaning of 'God's kingdom on earth' in and through his own person, in what he said and what he did.

There is no question that those who met Jesus saw him as one through whom the power and effect of God were dramatically at work. This was so striking that the Greek word *dunamis* was used to describe it, the word that underlies our own words 'dynamite' and 'dynamic'. Even his enemies did not deny that something extraordinary was happening in and through the person of Jesus: they simply said that he must be doing it through the power of the devil, Beelzebub, in order to seduce Jews from their true obedience to God.

So God's power was brought to vivid life by Jesus, but he never claimed to do any of those memorable things out of his own ability or strength: always he said that they came to him from God whom he called Father. When, therefore, the first followers of Jesus saw or heard him, it seemed to be God who was speaking and acting through him in ways that went far beyond ordinary human power. Crazy though it sounded, it seemed as though they had met God in Galilee.

The Crucifixion and the Resurrection

If Jesus had stayed in Galilee, we might not have heard much more about him. He would have been someone who offered an interesting and independent understanding of what the Covenant life with God should be. There were plenty of other teachers and wonder-workers in Galilee at that time (like Honi, the rainmaker) who have disappeared into the footnotes of history. But Jesus was again insistently different and independent in taking his understanding of God to Jerusalem, the only place at that time where, in the Temple, its truth and validity could be judged and decided. He was accused of threatening the Temple by his private and independent teaching, an offence that must, according to *Deuteronomy* 17, be punished by execution because such teaching would destroy Israel. Jesus was therefore handed over to the Romans, who alone could execute criminals, and he was crucified.

And that too might have been the end of the story. The fundamental question, therefore, is why the followers of Jesus (those who believed that they had met God in Galilee) continued to believe that this executed criminal was indeed 'the Christ'. Jesus himself had resisted (though he did not entirely exclude) beliefs that he spoke and acted as he did because he was the Messiah. Instead he called himself 'the son of man', a phrase (not a title) which, from its use in the Bible, meant, 'a man who has to die like all others but who will be rescued and vindicated by God'. He did certainly die but he was not rescued. On the Cross he cried out, 'My God, my God, why have you forsaken me?'

So how could those early followers believe that he was the promised Christ? The answer is that although they knew beyond doubt that he had died on the Cross, they knew with equal certainty, according to their own account, that he was alive after death. At first they could hardly believe it, and yet they were challenged by the witness of several people, not only that the tomb in which the body of Jesus had been laid was empty, but also that they had seen Jesus alive. Increasing numbers were persuaded, not least because they found that the *dunamis* of God (the consequence and effect of God) which they had experienced in his company was still dramatically at work among them.

The actual resurrection is not described, only the appearances of Jesus to a number of different people. The one whom they met was unmistakably Jesus, but in a form that was not in any way like that of a resuscitated body. Some, it is true, have argued that the resurrection cannot possibly have happened, saying, for example, that Jesus did not die on the cross but was taken down and revived, or that he died but that his followers could not forget him and were sure that his teaching and inspiration were still alive in them.

Those attempts to explain away the resurrection are unlikely because they do not explain the most obvious historical fact of all, the fact of the New Testament: what brought those unique and extraordinary documents into being? The stubborn historical fact of the New Testament is that it exists. Among all the many writings of the ancient world, the New Testament is unique: it contains lives and letters that resemble those written in the Greek world, and apocalyptic that is like other Jewish works of that kind. But each of the New Testament writings is completely different, because it is a consequence of the unique and utterly different life, and death, and, as they believed, life beyond death, of Jesus. It is a consequence also of the way in which the lives of those who had known Jesus were totally transformed by the one whom they had previously called 'Teacher', and whom they now call, 'My Lord and my God'—the response of one of the disciples, Thomas, who had scorned the possibility that Jesus might be alive after death until he also saw him and was convinced (see Figure 4).

The early Christians also called Jesus 'Christ' (Messiah) because he was for them and for others 'the conduit through whom the blessings of God flow' (to quote the phrase used of the Messiah in Chapter 3). The immense impact that Jesus had made on those who met him continued after he had died. Beyond his crucifixion and resurrection, the power and consequence of God, which through Jesus had changed the lives of so many, were no longer limited to those who happened to have met him in Galilee or in

God

4. This carving in the cloister of Santo Domingo de Silos, in northern Spain, shows the Apostles with Thomas (who had doubted the Resurrection) verifying that Jesus is risen from the dead

Judaea: they were made universal—as he had intended and put into effect on the night before he died.

Jesus went to Jerusalem on that last occasion to celebrate the Passover meal, the occasion when Jews remember the way in which God rescued them in the Exodus from Egypt. He knew that God through him had spoken and acted with equal power (*dunamis*) in ways that had changed the lives of others for good. But he knew also that his way of living and teaching had put his life in danger because of its challenge to the Temple authorities. He made clear to his close disciples that he did not expect to eat with them again on earth.

At the meal he tried to convey to his disciples that although he was about to die, nevertheless he would continue to be with them, so that all they had experienced through him of God's effect and consequence (*dunamis*) would continue. That seemed such a wild idea that the disciples could not understand what he meant. Jesus therefore put his words into actions of the kind that in those days prophets used to perform when they needed to bring home to people the urgency of their message. It was believed that these actions made some future event certain.

Jesus therefore took bread and said, 'This is my body that is for you: do this in remembrance of me', and he took a cup containing wine and said, 'This cup is the new covenant in my blood: do this as often as you drink it, in remembrance of me.'

The exact words that Jesus said are uncertain because the Gospels and Paul record them with slight differences. Nevertheless, they make it clear that Jesus, knowing what awaited him, created a new Covenant in which the relationship established through him with God in the present will continue in the future 'as often as . . ., as often as' (the words are repeated in *I Corinthians* 11.24f.) they do this in remembrance of him.

Jesus made that promise of his continuing presence not just for the disciples on that occasion, but, as *Mark* 14.24 puts it, 'for many' (i.e., for an immense multitude). Christians subsequently have found the promise to be true, but Jesus did not explain how it would happen. As a result, there have been many different understandings of what is happening when Christians gather to commemorate Jesus at the Last Supper, ranging from the belief that the bread and wine become the Body and Blood of Christ, to the belief that the bread and wine represent his Body and Blood.

What is common to them all is that the repeating of the words and actions of Jesus connects believers to the intention and promise of Jesus to be with them 'even to the end of the world' and to be a real and continuing presence in their midst.

The Son of God

Because the followers of Jesus found all this to be true, they called Jesus, not only Christ, but also the Son of God. The phrase 'the son of God' may have meant at that time simply 'one who obeys the calling of God'. But Jesus was called 'the Son of God' in a much stronger sense: one who is in a uniquely close relationship with God. They believed that this man, with whom they had lived and whom they knew so well, was God in their midst.

Some have thought that all this came much later in Christian belief—that an ordinary teacher and healer was gradually promoted until, as time passed, he became the Son of God. That is certainly wrong. From the *earliest* writings onwards of the New Testament, including the letters of Paul written only a few years after the crucifixion, the highest status and titles are given to Jesus, so that 'at the name of Jesus every knee should bend...and every tongue should confess that Jesus Christ is Lord' (*Philemon* 2.10f.). *Colossians* 1 (probably by Paul but some question this) writes of Jesus Christ as Lord, calling him 'the image of the invisible God, the firstborn of all creation; for in him all things in heaven and on earth were created.... All things have been created through him and for him. He himself is before all things, and in him all things hold together' (*Colossians* 1.15). The early writings still call him by his human name, Jesus, but they were written from a belief that Jesus was the self-expression of God, the Word of God, who had dwelt among them, full of grace and truth (*John* 1.14).

Already, therefore, within a few years of the crucifixion the early Christians were associating Jesus with God so closely that the adoration and worship due to God are due also to Jesus. They believed that the death of Jesus had been an act of God in dealing with and defeating the power of sin and death. Those are extraordinary claims to make about a crucified man, and the history of the early Church shows the first Christians struggling to understand the implications of what has happened.

The first and most obvious implication is that the Jewish understanding of God continues. The fundamental understanding of God as One, the Creator of all things and of all people, who called Israel to a particular service and obedience on behalf of the whole world, did not change, nor did the understanding of God as the sovereign Lord or Ruler who has command and control of all the nations.

What *did* change for them, as a consequence of Jesus believed to be the Christ, was their understanding of who God is and of how God is related to the world. For them the dream of the prophets was suddenly and surprisingly coming true—the dream that the day will come 'when the earth will be filled with the knowledge of the Lord as the waters cover the Sea' (*Isaiah* 11.9; *Habakkuk* 2.14). The purpose of God to bring to Israel healing, judgement, forgiveness, and redemption is through Christ extended to the whole world—it is, in other words, universalized.

The unfolding of doctrine: Christology, Atonement, and the Trinity

The universalizing through Jesus of God's Covenant and purpose to all people raised very large questions about the relationship between Jesus and God. Jesus in Galilee and Judaea had brought the effect of God unmistakably into many lives in many different ways. But he had insisted that these things were done and spoken, not by himself out of his own strength, but by God (whom he called Father) working through him. The first followers of Jesus had 'seen with their own eyes and touched with their own hands' (*I John* 1.1) one who embodied the truth and consequence of God in a unique and unmistakable way—far beyond anything achieved by the teachers and healers of the time with whom they were familiar.

The immediate question, therefore, was this: how could God be wholly present in and through this human person without compromising or overwhelming that humanity, the reality of which was demonstrated by his death on a cross? In later language, it was the question of how Jesus could be both truly God and yet wholly human.

That is the question of what is known as Christology, reflection on the person and nature of Christ. In the end (after centuries of debate and argument which continue to the present-day) it was widely accepted in Christian belief that Jesus united in one Person two distinct natures, that of God and that of humans, without compromising what it means to be God and without obliterating what it means to be human. Jesus thus embodied the reality of God (that 'embodiment' is known from the Latin *in carne* as 'the Incarnation'), not just in a few of his better moments, but constantly. As *Hebrews* 4.15 put it, Jesus was someone 'who in every respect has been tested as we are, yet without sin'.

For everyone else, however, sin (the things that people do that are wrong, the gap between humans and God) remains one of the facts of life. If people are to be reconciled to God and to each other, sin has to be dealt with and the gap closed. According to the story in *Genesis* 3.1–19, death is a consequence of the disobedience of Adam and Eve which also estranges them from God—they are banished from Eden and they can no longer meet up with God walking in the garden in the cool of the evening breeze (*Genesis* 3.8). Christians came to believe that God's embodied participation in the crucifixion and resurrection had inflicted a decisive defeat on death. It had destroyed the power of death over humanity and had therefore done for humans what they could not possibly do for themselves. The banishment from Eden is over, and people are made once more 'at one' with God. The Cross, therefore, in Christian belief achieves for ever and for all what the Day of Atonement achieved year by year in particular circumstances: the 'at-one-ment' with God is universalized.

But how? That is the question of Atonement. How can that death on the Cross affect others, countless others both before and after the time of Jesus, and achieve their atonement? In the New Testament many answers are suggested, mainly in metaphors drawn from the world in which they lived at that time. The efficacy of sacrifice in the Temple supplied one such metaphor, and *Hebrews* argues that Christians now have even better sacrifices (9.23), a better High Priest (4.14–6) and a better covenant (8.6). Another metaphor was the price that has to be paid if slaves are to be bought and then set free. Another was the acceptance on behalf of an offender of the due penalty for an offence, which then allows the charge, not to be ignored or overlooked, but to be cancelled altogether. Another was to see Christ as victorious over death, as Christus Victor. That connects to the story in *Genesis*, contrasting the first Adam (who passes on to his descendants the penalty of death) with Christ as the second Adam who destroys death and passes on to those who will receive it the gift of eternal life—a life immersed 'in Christ' that begins in the metaphorical death of baptism and is already experienced now, so that Christians, as Paul put it, 'are *already*

dead because their life lies hidden with Christ in God'
(*Colossians* 3.3).

Those two questions (of Christology and of Atonement) then
raised an obvious third question: what does all this imply about
the nature and being of God? How can God be wholly present in
the person of Jesus and yet still be running the universe? And how
at the same time can God be actively at work in people and events
all over the world? The Bible constantly describes that activity and
speaks of it particularly in terms of the breath or the spirit of God:
the breath of God inspires (Latin *in* + *spiro*, 'I breathe') people
such as prophets, it fills others, such as Bezalel, with 'ability,
intelligence and knowledge' (*Exodus* 31.3), and it urges others,
such as Othniel (*Judges* 3.10), to go to war.

The Hebrew word for 'spirit' is *ruach* which may simply mean
'breath' or 'wind', so that *Genesis* 1.2, translated in the Authorized
Version as 'the Spirit of God moved upon the face of the waters',
might equally be translated as 'a wind from God swept over the
face of the waters'. Increasingly, however, *ruach* was identified as
the personal agent of God in the world, God in urgency and
effect. Christians were faced with the question of how the three,
Creator, Redeemer and Spirit, belong together as the one reality
of God.

That is the question of the Trinity. There could not be any
compromise on *yihud haShem*, on the Oneness of God. That was
absolute and non-negotiable. In the case of God, there can only be
what God is. Why then did Christians come to believe that the
nature of God must be Triune (Three in One)?

The Christian understanding of God as Trinity begins at the
only place where any knowledge of God *can* begin, in the ways
in which life is experienced in a universe of this kind including
what are taken to be the effects and consequences of God. On
that basis, Christians have had no option but to understand God

as One who is active in creating and sustaining all things; who is active in seeking to find, to recover, and to renew that which was lost; who is active in inspiring the transformations of human life and relationships in so many different and often surprising ways.

In the language of the time, they spoke of God as Father (the Creator of life, time and history), as Son (the Redeemer), as the Holy Spirit (who turns people into gifted children—those who receive all things as gift from God and who show their thankfulness in faith, hope, and love). But those Three cannot be three gods or three bits of God, as we have seen. They can only be what God is in essence, in whom that Triune relatedness is what that essence is. The Father is the source of the Son through whom the action of the Holy Spirit draws human beings into that essential and eternal relatedness in the process known as *theosis*, 'divinization'—being made, that is, participants in the interior dynamic and being of God.

No doubt it sounds complicated. The physicist John Wheeler once observed that if you are not completely confused by quantum mechanics you do not understand it—and Niels Bohr himself maintained that if you are not shocked when you first come across quantum theory, you cannot possibly have understood it. The same is true of the Trinity—not surprisingly, because God is unlikely to be easier to understand than an aspect of creation like quantum mechanics, and because also God is not going to be contained within the limits of human understanding.

It was easy, therefore, for the so-called Athanasian Creed (a 5th century summary of Christian faith that attained wide authority) to say that 'whoever wishes to be saved must…worship one God in the Trinity and the Trinity in unity, without either confusing the persons or dividing the substance', but it has proved impossible to reach agreement on how that minimal statement about 'what God is' can be understood.

Even so, at least something can be said about those ways in which the Trinity has become known or at least discernible by faith. If we begin with our experience of 'the Beyond in our midst', as Bonhoeffer put it, we are led to what is known as the 'economic' Trinity. The Greek word *oikonomia* (underlying the English word 'economy') is made up of *oikos*, 'home' + *nomos*, 'law' or 'regulation'; so the phrase 'economic Trinity' refers to God's dealings with the universe and with humanity, and it concentrates on the Immanence of God in the sense already discussed in Chapter 1.

It is then possible to draw inferences from 'the economic Trinity' to what the being of God must be in itself (Latin *in se* or *a se*, so that the essential Being of God, 'what God is', is known as the aseity of God)—but they, like all abductive inferences, must be tentative. To make matters even more confusing, this reflection on the inner Being of God also uses the word 'immanent'. 'The immanent Trinity' in *this* sense is asking how the threefold nature of God in creation, salvation, and sanctification ('the economic Trinity') is related to the eternal and Transcendent Being of God ('the immanent Trinity'). The question is possible because 'the economic Trinity' must logically and actually express what God is: it cannot be something entirely different as though the fingerprint on a stone has no connection with the finger that pressed on it.

The inner being of God, therefore, must be in itself a unity constituted by interrelatedness—or to put it more simply, as the New Testament does put it (*I John* 4.8), 'God is love'. It is then possible to reflect inferentially on 'what God must be in order to be God' by beginning with the fingerprints in creation and in the experience of redemption and sanctification, all of which together draw people into the holiness and the love of God in a way that they can already begin to experience.

So the reflections on the immanent Trinity (on the aseity of God transcending the limits of space and time) arise from the transforming consequence of the economic Trinity in relation to ourselves. As Catherine LaCugna put it,

> Trinitarian theology is par excellence a theology of relationship: God to us, we to God, we to each other. The doctrine of the Trinity affirms that the 'essence' of God is relational, other-ward, that God exists as diverse persons united in a communion of freedom, love, and knowledge.

It is impossible here to follow the immense and often complicated debates in Christian history about Christology, Atonement and the Trinity—debates that continue to the present day. They proved so divisive that Christians frequently persecuted other Christians who had different views on these complicated matters, and they remain among the reasons why the Churches are still divided.

Christian beliefs about the relation of Jesus to the Father and about the Trinity are clearly different from the Jewish understanding and characterization of God, even though the Christian understanding is rooted in the Jewish Bible. It is a real and serious question, as Miroslav Volf has asked it, 'Do we worship the same God?' But whatever answer is given, both Christianity and Judaism came to be challenged themselves by another understanding of God which was derived from the same tradition but which saw itself as the true successor of both Christianity and Judaism. They were challenged by Islam.

Chapter 5

The religions of Abraham: Muslim understandings of God

> He is God. There is no God but He, the One who knows the hidden and the open. He is the merciful Lord of mercy. He is God. There is no God but He, the King, the holy One....He is God, the Creator, Maker, Designer. To God belong the most beautiful Names. All that is in the heavens and the earth declares the glory of God, the Mighty, the Wise. (Quran 59.22–4)

In those words, and many others like them, the Quran proclaims the sovereign majesty of God. In doing so it continues the message of the Prophets whom God has sent in the past: 'We have given revelation to you [Muhammad] as we gave revelation to Noah and the Prophets who came after him. We gave revelation to Abraham, Ishmael, Isaac, Jacob and the tribes, to Jesus, Job, Jonah, Aaron and Solomon, and to David we gave the Psalms' (4.163).

It follows, therefore, that the understanding and characterization of God in the Quran is not new. It cannot be, because God is eternal and unchanging and 'bears witness to himself' (4.166). Muhammad, as the prophet of God, transmits that witness to the world. That is why the Muslim understanding of God is summarized in the statement or 'witness' (Arabic *shahada*), 'There is no God but God, and Muhammad is his messenger.' To bear witness to God in that way is to be a Muslim, one who enters into that condition of obedience and safety in relation to God known as Islam.

The word for God in Arabic is Allah. It is made up from a contraction of the article *al*, 'the', and *ilah* which has connections with El and Elohim. In the close relation between Arabic and Hebrew that is not surprising, and it is likely that 'Allah' was intended to convey 'the One who *is* God'—as opposed to the many conflicting ideas about gods and goddesses.

Despite the close connections, many Muslims have insisted that in order to distinguish Muslim from Jewish and Christian characterizations of God, Allah should not be translated as 'God'. In 2013, a Malaysian Court of Appeal ruled that only Muslims can use 'Allah' despite its use in Arabia long before the time of Muhammad. Muslims recognize that to God belong 'the most beautiful Names', and they list 'the Ninety-nine Beautiful Names' beginning with The First, The Last, The One, but Allah is different because it points to the Essence (*al-Dhat*), the aseity (to pick up the technical word used earlier) of God.

Muhammad

Islam began historically with the life and work of Muhammad who lived in Arabia 570–632, but from the Muslim point of view Islam began long before that. It began with the purpose of God in Creation that people should live according to what is known as Din. The word *din* is conventionally translated as 'religion' (as in this book), but it needs to be remembered that in Muslim understanding Din embraces the whole of life: there cannot be a distinction between 'religious' and 'secular'. Muhammad understood himself to be a prophet sent by God to call people back to that lifeway of faith and behaviour which recognizes God in gratitude and lives as God desires—and commands.

But called back from what? From false understandings of God, and from the wrong beliefs and behaviours that follow from false understanding. They were not difficult to find in Arabia at the time when Muhammad was born. In his birthplace, Mecca, there were many different ways of characterizing and worshipping God: there were substantial communities of Jews and Christians, and Mecca itself was a pilgrimage centre for the worship of local deities (including Hubal, god of the moon, and the goddesses alUzza, Manat and al-Lat), who were worshipped through images known in English as 'idols' (Greek *eidola*).

In and around Mecca at that time there were some people (known as the Hanifs) who admired the moral life of the Jews and who saw why, following the Jews with their emphasis on the Oneness of God, they must totally reject idolatry. The Hanifs, therefore, were trying to follow 'the religion of Ibrahim' (the Arabic form of Abraham). Among them was Zayid ibn Amr, who condemned the worship of idols in Mecca and who used to pray, 'O God, I do not know how you desire to be worshipped, but if I did know, I would worship as you desire.' He rebuked Muhammad for worshipping idols, and Muhammad said later, 'After that, I never willingly touched idols [to receive power from them], nor did I offer sacrifices to them.'

Instead, Muhammad (like other Hanifs) went off on his own to a cave on Mount Hira where, in complete isolation, he sought to find God as God truly is—to find what he called alHaqq, literally 'the True' (one of the Beautiful Names). It was there on one occasion that he had the overwhelming experience of one (whom he later identified as Jibril or Gabriel) who was pressing on him and commanding him three times, *Iqra*, 'recite' (cf., *Miqra*, a Hebrew word for Tanach). From that stunning and overwhelming experience began the occasions throughout the rest of his life when he felt the pressure to recite the words that now stand in the Quran—*alQuran* is derived from the same root as *iqra*. For Muslims, therefore, the answer to the question, 'Who or what is God?', is given clearly and decisively in the Quran.

The Quran

Muhammad is not in any sense the author of a book called 'the Quran'. He was, as he and others believed, the recipient of words received from God which he then transmitted into the world. 'The Mother of the Book' (*umm alKitab*, 43.3f.) is with God in heaven, and it was, in Muslim belief, simply sent down and given to Muhammad in Arabic. That is why Arabic is so precious as a language, and why many Muslims learn to recite the Quran by heart, even if they do not understand Arabic, because it brings the powerful blessing (*baraka*) of God.

After the death of Muhammad, there were some (especially the Mutazilites, in the 8th and 9th centuries) who reasoned that the Quran must have been *created* (i.e., brought into being) for specific circumstances since it mentions people and events. But the contrary view prevailed that 'the Quran is the speech of God, written in copies, preserved in memories, recited in speech, revealed to the Prophet. Our pronouncing, writing and reciting the Quran is created, but the Quran itself is uncreated.' Later, it was believed that if the Quran is uncreated, then so too must be its recitation.

In Muslim belief, therefore, the Quran is the uncorrupted, complete and final revelation transmitted from God through Muhammad into the world. It is true that al-Shaytan (Satan) tried to corrupt the Quran by whispering words into Muhammad's ear, as when he made Muhammad say to the Meccans that their goddesses might be regarded as intercessors carrying messages to God. Those were the original 'Satanic verses', but when Muhammad recognized their origin they were repudiated. Meccan idolatry could not be accommodated, it had to be destroyed.

That repudiation is an example of what is known as 'abrogation' (*naskh*) in which one part of the Quran is suppressed, developed or replaced by a later part. It is still, however, God's act and not a human intervention, and it does not affect the belief that the Quran is the literal word of God. That belief, however, raised other problems of its own, particularly of the extent to which the words of the Quran may or may not be understood metaphorically. For example, the Quran states that God is 'firmly established on the throne' (e.g., 7.52/4, 10.3): does that imply that God sits literally on a throne?

In the arguments about the Attributes of God, the literalists claimed that the Quran as the Word of God must be describing 'what God is like', and they were known as *alMushabbiha*, 'the Likeners': God must be 'established on the throne', but in God's own way. Their opponents quoted the Quran against them (e.g., 42.9, 'There is nothing like God') and claimed that the offence of saying that God is in any way 'like humans' (*tashbih*) is almost as disastrous as associating anything with God as though it is God (*shirk*). Some looked instead for metaphorical or allegorical meanings, but ibn Hanbal (d. 855) led the way in resisting efforts to bring God within the limits of human reason and understanding. He argued, instead, that God can be known only through Revelation in the terms through which God chooses— including such terms as face, hands, throne. We cannot know what God is 'in essence' (*binafsihi*; cf. *a se / in se*, defined earlier), so we have to use those and similar descriptive words but 'without asking how' (*bila kayf*) they are to be applied.

Arguments of this nature did not affect the belief that the Quran is the transmission into the world of the Mother of the Book in heaven. The Quran, therefore, makes God and the will of God so clearly known that it becomes the non-negotiable foundation of Muslim belief and behaviour. But as with Torah, so also here: the Quran does not deal with every aspect of life, particularly as the world constantly changes, so the Quran has to be interpreted and applied. Of decisive authority in doing this were the many Traditions, known collectively as Hadith, recording the things that Muhammad said and did (and his silences).

On the basis of Quran and Hadith, different schools of Sharia emerged. *Sharia* meant originally 'the path that camels follow to the watering place', and the schools of Sharia organize a detailed account of the path that Muslims should follow in their lives. The Schools differ among themselves, with some being more rigorous and literalistic than others, but in the context of Sharia, Muslims can know exactly how to live in the constant presence of God. The constancy of that presence is secured through Dhikr, the 'remembrance of God' commanded in the Quran as a deliberate focus on God, called by Muhammad 'the best act of worship'.

Muslims realize, of course, that they frequently fail in many different ways—the Quran has more than a hundred different words for human fault or sin—but God is believed fundamentally to be merciful. The Quran itself opens with the words, 'In the name of God, the merciful Lord of mercy.' That is why, as an act of mercy, God repeatedly sends prophets to remind people of the right way to behave and believe, and to recall them to the correction of their erring ways. That self-correction is urgent because at the final judgement of all people on the Last Day, God will weigh each person's deeds on an exact balance, and will reward or punish them accordingly.

The People of the Book

The preexistent and uncreated Quran means, in Muslim belief, that all previous messengers or prophets delivered or transmitted the same message from God, even though it was related contingently to the circumstances of their own time. Thus the Quran mentions specific battles that were contingent to the life of Muhammad, but the lessons to be drawn from victory or from defeat are not contingent: they are timeless. Among those earlier prophets who transmitted the same message were Moses (Musa) and Jesus (Isa), and the Quran includes Jewish and Christian stories—though not as they are recorded in Tanach and the New Testament.

Muhammad thus believed himself to be the latest in a long line of prophets, but he came to be regarded as the *last* of the prophets, and he is known by Muslims as 'the Seal of the Prophets'. That claim rests on the belief that in the case of all previous prophets, people confused and corrupted the message (the Quran) by mixing it up with all sorts of other material—stories, for example, about the prophets, so that the Christian Gospels contain the same message but mixed up with stories about Jesus and the disciples.

In Muslim belief, the Quran is completely different because it was never confused with anything else—not even with the words that Muhammad spoke, which are always recorded separately in Hadith. They have great authority in Islam but they are never confused with the Quran. Even the Hadith that record words spoken by God (known distinctively as Hadith Qudsi) are not confused with the Quran.

Those who have received the Quran in the past, no matter how much they have mistreated it, are recognized as such. They are called Ahl alKitab, 'the People of the Book', and Muslims are required by the Quran to respect them. Muhammad himself said, 'Anyone who does wrong to a Jew or a Christian will find me as his accuser on the day of judgement.' But at the same time, when Jews and Christians refused to recognize Muhammad as a prophet in the long line of their own prophets, and when some among them rejected Muhammad and fought against him, Muslims are told in the Quran (and this an example of abrogation responding to changed contingent conditions) to fight in defence against them.

Although, therefore, the Quran allows, and, for some Muslims, commands, confrontation in some specific circumstances, there have been long periods when Muslims, Jews, and Christians have lived, not just in peace with each other, but in works of cooperation, not least in science and scholarship. There is of course much in the Quranic characterization of God that Jews and

Christians would recognize, not least the uncompromising insistence on the Oneness of God. Oneness (*tawhid*; cf., *ahad*, 'one', Hebrew *ehad*) is fundamental in Muslim belief. So Ruthven claims, 'If there is a single word that can be taken to represent the primary impulse of Islam, be it theological, political, or sociological, it is *tawhid*.' The Sura of Unity (112; called *Ikhlas*: suras are the sections of the Quran moving, generally speaking, from the longest to the shortest) is so fundamental and profound that those who say it with conviction shed their sins as a tree in autumn sheds its leaves:

> Say: He is God, alone [*ahad*], God the absolute. He does not beget, he is not begotten, and there is none in any way equal to him.

In that context, however, Christian language *taken literally* of a Father and an 'only-begotten Son' is impossible—and, taken literally, Christians would obviously agree. But Muslim questions about the Trinity appear, as David Thomas has shown, 'from the earliest times': how can 'God the absolute' have a wife and son, and how can three distinct Persons nevertheless be One? In Muslim belief, it is the Quran alone that reveals the nature and character of God, just as it reveals what individuals, families, and societies must believe and how they must behave.

The Will of God

According to the Quran (e.g., 81.27–9), humans have the responsibility as an act of will to follow 'the straight path', but they cannot will to do that unless God wills them to do so. It is thus the responsibility of Muslims to put into effect the will of God on earth. This is expressed in the commonly heard phrase, *insh' Allah*, 'if God wills it'.

Muslims seek to discern God's will on the basis of Quran and Hadith, in the context of Sharia, but that does not mean that they all live in exactly the same way or that they necessarily agree on how the will of God is to be implemented. The divisions between Sunni and Shia Muslims are obvious at the present time, but even among Sunni Muslims we have seen that there are four major schools of Sharia, each of which has its own understanding of how literally the life of Muhammad and his Companions must be reproduced and imitated in the present day.

To give another example, many Muslims are Sufis who seek to draw close to God in devotion and obedience. Sufis are those who seek direct and personal experience of God, but there are many schools or traditions of Sufi training and practice which are very different from each other. Even so, their common purpose was summarized by one of the greatest of them, the poet and teacher Rumi: 'My religion is to live through love.' As he died at sunset in December 1273, he said, 'My death is my wedding with eternity.'

Sufis not only differed among themselves, they were often regarded with suspicion by other Muslims who thought that they might be abandoning Sharia. Eventually alGhazali (d. 1111) showed how the Sufi way of devotion is rooted in Sharia, and how philosophy, theology and the Sufi way belong together. 'What it means to be a Sufi,' he wrote, 'is to live unceasingly in union with God and at peace with all people.' By reconciling the tensions between the three he came to be called *Hujjat alIslam*, the proof of Islam.

There are, therefore, many different forms and interpretations of Islam. What is common to them all is the belief that the answer to the question, 'Who or what is God?' is given by God in the Quran. There it is made clear that creation, the events of history and the outcomes in individual lives come from God and remain in the control and determination of God:

> He is the first and the last, the manifest and the hidden, and he knows all things.
>
> He it is who created the heavens and the earth in six days, then he established himself on the Throne. He knows what enters into

the earth and what comes forth from it, what comes down from heaven and what goes up to it. He is with you wherever you are and he sees whatever you do.

His is the sovereign authority [literally, 'kingship'] over the heavens and the earth, and to God every matter returns.

He moves night into day and day into night, and he has full knowledge of the contents of the heart. (57.3–6)

The absolute power of God to determine all things is known as Qadr. But how can that be reconciled with human freedom and moral responsibility? If God determines all things, how can individuals be held responsible on the Last Day, the Day of Judgement? The philosophizing Mutazilites believed in 'man's self-sufficiency, in his power to control his life, and earn Paradise for himself, and it was coupled with the belief in the complete competence of human reason'.

But that view was rejected by the ongoing majority of Muslims for whom the absolute sovereignty of God is so unequivocal in the Quran that God must create or originate every act and thought. It was believed, therefore, that God creates all the possibilities and delegates to individuals the responsibility to choose from among the possibilities—the doctrine of 'acquisition' or *kasb/iktisab*: God wills and creates all human actions, but humans are still morally responsible for acquiring them: 'All things that people do, whether moving or resting, are undoubtedly their own acquisition [*kasb*], but it is God who creates them, and they are brought into being by the will, the knowledge, the decision and the decree of God.'

By exercising that responsibility and by living in the way commanded by God in the Quran, Muslims can have trust in God whose nature is always to have mercy—exactly as *alFatiha*, 'The Opening' (see Figure 5), the first sura of the Quran, states:

بِسْمِ اللهِ الرَّحْمَنِ الرَّحِيمِ ❋

❋ الْحَمْدُ لِلهِ رَبِّ الْعَالَمِينَ ❋ الرَّحْمَنِ الرَّحِيمِ ❋

❋ مَلِكِ يَوْمِ الدِّينِ ❋ إِيَّاكَ نَعْبُدُ وَإِيَّاكَ نَسْتَعِينُ ❋

❋ اهْدِنَا الصِّرَاطَ الْمُسْتَقِيمَ ❋ صِرَاطَ الَّذِينَ

أَنْعَمْتَ عَلَيْهِمْ غَيْرِ الْمَغْضُوبِ عَلَيْهِمْ وَلا

الضَّالِّينَ ❋

5. The Opening Sura of the Quran, alFatiha

In the name of God, the merciful Lord of mercy.
Praise be to God, the Lord of all being,
The merciful Lord of mercy,
Sovereign of the Day of Judgement:
You alone do we serve and to You alone we come for help:
Guide us in the straight path,
The path of those on whom You have bestowed favour,
Not of those against whom is the wrath,
Nor of those who are straying in error.

There are many ways of 'straying in error', but the worst among
them is *shirk* (already mentioned). In practice, it is the fundamental
offence of idolatry, the worship of gods in the form of idols against
which Muhammad fought until he destroyed the idols of Mecca.
When their conquests led Muslims to India (8th century onwards),
they found what they believed to be a comparable idolatry among
the Hindus. Images of gods and goddesses were so pervasive that
a widespread Muslim tradition claims that idolatry began in India
and was taken from there to Arabia. They could not ignore the
command of God to destroy idols wherever they found them.

A historian of the 12th century, Ziya udDin Barani, recorded 'a fanatical preacher' at the court of the Delhi Sultan:

> They [rulers] have an obligation to create a safe refuge for the faith, and that obligation cannot be met until, for the sake of God and the protection of the true Din, they have completely destroyed defiance and unbelief, polytheism and idolatry. If rulers cannot wholly eradicate, either polytheism and defiance because they are deep-rooted, or the infidels and polytheists because they are so numerous, it will still count as meritorious if, for the sake of Islam and of creating safe refuge for the true Din, they do their best to insult and humiliate, to distress, ridicule and belittle the Hindus who are polytheists and worshippers of idols.

There were other Muslims, not least the emperor Akbar (1542–1605), who were more positive about Indian beliefs, and some have sought to include them as a People of the Book. But are those Muslims right who have regarded Hindus as 'polytheists and worshippers of idols'? Is that a true description of Indian beliefs about God?

Chapter 6
Religions of India

The India that Muslims entered was not a single entity, except in the religious sense that the whole of India was regarded as a holy place connected by its myriad places of pilgrimage. Even then, the religious beliefs and practices of Indians were extremely diverse. That is why the term 'Hinduism' to describe Indian religion can be misleading. The word *hindu* appeared in Persian to describe those who live beyond the river Indus (Sanskrit *sindhu*). The term 'Hinduism' was introduced by the British in the 19th century to describe the religion and civilization of the Indian subcontinent, but it is misleading if it implies uniformity in belief and practice.

Some basic beliefs

In fact and in contrast, Indian religion is more like a large family with many different members. There are family resemblances of overriding importance, and the different members of the family therefore hold much in common. For example, they believe (that is, now; these beliefs were not held in early times) that the enduring and immortal self (called Atman) in each individual is not other than 'that which truly is', Brahman, the source of all appearance. Atman is reborn in many lives through the chain of rebirth (Samsara), until it finds its way to release (Mukti or Moksha). The process of Samsara may be a very long one (perhaps many millions of lives), and it is governed by Karma. Karma is a natural law in the moral world producing outcomes in rebirth for better or for worse as certainly as the natural laws in the physical world (like gravity) produce predictable outcomes. Karma leads to consequence through the process of rebirth. Rebirth as a human is the rare opportunity to break the sequence of rebirth, thus attaining Moksha, release.

So the 'family members' share many beliefs however much they may be differently interpreted. Where those different interpretations become organized they are known as Sampradayas, 'traditions'. The differences between them can be serious, and they can lead to what we might call 'family rows'—rivalries and disagreements, as a result of which some of the family members have in the past taken themselves off to establish a life of their own. Jains and Buddhists are early examples that have in effect become separate religions (for reasons, as we will see, that arise from the Indian understanding of God). Even so, the remaining and continuing family members still regard them as part of the family. In their classification of the philosophical systems in India, six are regarded as legitimate (*astika*), while three, including Jains and Buddhists, are regarded as *nastika*, outsiders, because they deny the divine origin of the Vedas (the status and relation of the Vedas to the divine are described later in this chapter).

From all this, it follows that Indian understandings and characterizations of God are extremely diverse and certainly cannot be summarized even in a very long introduction, let alone in a short one. That diversity, far from being a matter of regret, is fundamental and necessary in the Indian understanding of God. It will lead us to see that the equation 'India = idolatry' is profoundly mistaken.

The immense diversity that exists in the Indian imagination of God is expressed in the vivid proliferation of worship, rituals, meditation, music, art, architecture, and so on, but it is held together in the context, not just of certain fundamental beliefs, but in the wide acceptance of common practice and social organization known collectively as 'Dharma'. That is why a common Indian name for what has come to be called 'Hinduism' is Sanatana Dharma, 'everlasting Dharma'. Dharma in this context means, roughly, 'appropriate behaviour'—behaviour, that is, which is appropriate for every circumstance on the part of the person or the people involved. As such, it is, for example, the Dharma of a soldier to fight even though Ahimsa, non-violence and respect for life, is a paramount virtue.

Sanatana Dharma is a kind of 'map' of the appropriate behaviour underlying the different ways in which individuals can make progress in order to escape for ever from the chain of Samsara, rebirth. The 'ways' are known as Marga, and they are gathered together in the Three Ways (Trimarga) that lead to liberation. The first two are Karmamarga, the way of action including the rituals and sacrifices that lead to purity of life; and Jnanamarga, the way of knowledge, insight, and understanding. The third is Bhaktimarga, the way of loving devotion to God.

Worship and seeing God

So we return to the question with which we began: who or what is God? In India a beginning of an answer lies in the opportunity that people have to meet God directly. As Diana Eck has observed, 'encountering God' (the title of her book) is not difficult in India: '[T]here is nothing in the substance of this world that cannot display the presence and glory of God—an enlightened person, a cow, a tree, a basil bush, even a lump of clay.'

Among the enlightened people, gurus play a key role. Gurus are guides to God, the latest usually in a long line of tradition, and some are regarded as the actual embodiment of God. Beside gurus, there are many ways and many places in India where God is brought to people (and people are brought to God) through forms of manifestation. God can be approached and discerned through forms of appearance—of which the many images (known as *murti*, 'embodiment') of God, particularly in Temples and on their walls, are an example. Each is in its way an epiphany. The Greek word *epiphaneia* means 'manifestation'—as in the Feast of the Epiphany when Christians believe that God was made manifest in Christ.

In India, the epiphanies of God are everywhere for those who have the eyes to see them. A key word for 'worship' is *darshan*, which means 'seeing'. The ceremonial acts of worship are called Puja, but the engagement with God is Darshan, a direct 'seeing and being seen', as the art historian Stephen Huyler puts it:

> Puja is the ceremonial act of showing reverence to a God or Goddess through invocation, prayer, song, and ritual. An essential aspect of puja for Hindus is communion with the Divine. The worshipper believes that with this contact she or he has established direct contact with the deity. Most often that contact is facilitated through an image: an element of nature, a sculpture, vessel, painting, or print. When the image is consecrated at the time of its installation in a shrine or temple, the deity is invited to invest the image with his or her cosmic energy. . . . The principal aim of any puja is this feeling of personal contact with the deity. Darshan, literally translated from Sanskrit as 'seeing and being seen by God', is that moment when the worshipper is receptive to recognition by the God or Goddess. Darshan may be achieved in a variety of ways, [but] through whatever means it comes, darshan brings both peace and blessing to Hindu devotees, and through it, they believe, miracles can and do occur frequently.

There are thus many forms in and through which the epiphanies of God are given visual expression, and superficially (on the surface of the many images) it may look like polytheistic idolatry. But these visible forms of epiphany are a means to the End that lies beyond themselves.

The epiphanies of 'God' (the unproduced Producer of all that is) go back to the Vedas (from *vid*, 'knowledge'), the earliest surviving texts of Indian religion: they emerged in northwest India from about 1500 BCE. The word 'emerged' reflects the belief that the texts were not written or composed by human authors (they are called *apaurusheya*, not made by humans), but are preexistent and are 'discerned' by Rishis, 'those who see'.

The Vedas and the Devas

Vedic religion was based on sacrifice and ritual to which the Vedas are related in different ways: some (notably the collection known as *Rig Veda*) collect hymns and chants used on ritual occasions, others give instructions on what has to be done, and others offer explanations and interpretations of what the sacrifices mean. The ritual experts who conducted and controlled the sacrifices were known as Brahmans (brahmins) so that the religion derived from the Vedas is often known as Brahmanism or Brahmanic religion.

The beings to whom the hymns and sacrifices are offered are known as Devas, heavenly beings who dwell in their own domain above those of atmosphere and earth. Deva is often translated as God, but the words *deva* and *devi* are related to *dyaus* (as in the Preface) and *daeva*, 'shining/exalted', and are used of many things that seem to have come from a more-than-human origin. It is certainly not a simple word meaning 'God'. The Devas have human emotions and desires, and they can be invited to the ritual meals that accompany the sacrifices which are offered to them.

The Devas are thus closely related to the world in which people lived at that time, and in particular to the natural phenomena that might help or hinder their survival. For example, one of the Devas, Agni, is related to fire; another, Aditi, to mother earth; another, Ushas, to the dawn and to the light and warmth of the sun: 'Come, Dawn, drive back the subterfuge of night.'

It was once thought that the Devas were personifications of natural phenomena, but that is far too simplistic. In Vedic belief, the primordial and undifferentiated Sound takes form and shape in the cosmos, much as we might say that energy derived from the Big Bang issues in the many different architectures of the universe. The Devas are different epiphanies of the primordial Origin who bring into effect the underlying and unfolding order of the cosmos. Even Indra, the highest of the Devas, is an epiphany of that kind taking many different forms of manifestation: Indra is called Pururupavat, 'having many forms', all of which are regarded as equal. The Devas, therefore, are in their different ways manifestations of the One. Sound becomes manifest as Word, known as Vac, and Vac is expressed through the other Devas: 'I [Vac] support Varuna and Mitra, I contain Indra, Agni and the Ashvins.'

This means that the Devas as epiphanies may be called by different names (and rightly so, since they manifest different energies in different forms), but they are expressions of 'that which is':

> They call it Indra, Mitra, Varuna,
> Agni and Garutman, the heavenly bird.
> Of the One the singers chant in many ways;
> They call it Agni, Yama, Matarishvan.

If the Devas are understood in that way, as epiphanies of the Primordial Origin, it is not surprising that none of them is in itself immutably fixed. That is why, as Brahmanic religion developed, there is a constant process of change and even displacement of one Deva by another, much as YHWH displaced El (see Chapter 3). Indra, Varuna and Rudra are all important in the Vedas but later lose their significance. Rudra simply becomes an epithet or description of Shiva who only appears in the Vedas as a word describing Rudra as 'the auspicious one'!

Even more dramatically, as Brahmanic religion spread from the northwest into the whole of India, the epiphanies of God in the

Vedas were associated with existing beliefs in the other parts of India, and this completely transformed the characterizations of God.

In south India that happened with far-reaching consequences for the understanding of God, particularly among the Tamils. To give an example, Tamils use the word *teyvam* to speak of all that lies within the nature of God. *Teyvam* becomes manifest in the many forms in which God appears, above all in Murukan, so-called because Murukan is the embodiment of *muruku*, the beauty and unageing loveliness that characterize *teyvam*. Brahmanic religion, when it reached south India, did not displace Murukan but tried to bring him, so to speak, 'into the family' by making him a son of Rudra known as Skanda. The Tamils, however, continued to regard Murukan as the One who is God; and they went so far as to call their own sacred texts 'the fifth Veda'.

That process of development and change is one, not so much of displacement, as of absorption, assimilation, and extension. It is known technically as 're-enculturation'. It was called more jauntily by Bharati 'the pizza effect', whereby 'a simple, hot-baked bread without trimmings' was taken from Calabria and Sicily to the US where it was transformed by the addition of elaborate toppings, and was returned to Italy as the changed meaning of 'pizza'.

That process produced the great characterizations of God in the form of Vishnu and Shiva. Together with Brahma they make up what is sometimes called 'the Hindu Trinity', with Brahma as Creator, Vishnu as Sustainer, and Shiva as Destroyer. As the manifest forms of God they mediate the recurring and constant cosmic process, the unending sequences of origin, rise, decline and destruction. It produced also Mahadevi, the Great Goddess who does for the Gods what they cannot do for themselves.

Vishnu and Shiva became immensely popular throughout India. Each of them attracted such large numbers of devotees that they developed into independent systems of belief and practice known as Vaishnavism and Shaivism. In contrast to Jains and Buddhists, however, they remained part of the family. Jains and Buddhists rejected the authority of the Vedas, and that carried with it a rejection of the Devas and of the belief that the sacrifices offered to them will make a difference. Neither Jainism nor Buddhism is atheistic. As the Buddhist scholar Marasinghe has observed, 'Early Buddhism found accommodation within its cosmological thinking for the gods that it adopted from contemporary religious thought', and later Buddhism added many more, to all of whom prayers and sacrifices are offered. What was rejected was any belief in 'an unproduced Producer of all that is', a Creator who exists independently from this or any other universe. Gods, like Devas or any other heavenly beings, are higher-level forms of appearance seeking, in the long process of reappearances, their own Enlightenment and release.

Vishnu

In contrast to Jains and Buddhists, followers of Vishnu (Vaishnavites) believe that Vishnu is the supreme Lord, Ishvara, who is utterly Transcendent but who pervades all things and is therefore Immanent and omnipresent: Vishnu is present in all humans as Antaryamin, the inner guide or controller. The Transcendent becomes manifest and Immanent in the visible form known as *arcavatara*, particularly in images (*murti*) and Temples. *Murti* means 'embodiment', and the ways in which images are made and then 'brought to life' and imbued with cosmic energy are governed by very careful rules. The presence may be permanent or for the moment of a particular ritual or act of worship.

'Embodiment' also occurs in the forms of manifestation known as *avatara*. Avatars are the epiphanies of God in living form, animal as well as human. The word *avatara* means 'descent', although it is often translated as 'incarnation'. In the case of Vishnu, there are many Avatars (including the Buddha) of whom a list of Ten (*dashavatara*) is recognized as preeminent, but the most revered among them are Rama and Krishna.

Rama is the hero of the great epic *Ramayana* whose words and actions exemplify the meaning of Dharma: Ayodhya, one of the seven sacred cities in India, was the home of Rama, hence the angry destruction in 1992 of a mosque built on the site of his Temple. Krishna is the focus of immense devotion and love—expressed consummately in the poetry of the Alvars in South India between roughly the 6th and 9th centuries:

> Look! You can see the servants of the Lord,
> Running, racing everywhere in crowds over the earth,
> Dancing and singing his praise.

The ecstasy of that love is glimpsed and anticipated in the consummation of love between a man and a woman, and it is exemplified in the love between Krishna and Radha, a union-in-relatedness between the divine and human that is the goal of devotion. It is through Krishna as Avatar that Vishnu reveals in *Bhagavadgita* the interrelatedness of the Three Ways that lead to freedom, of which Bhakti, loving devotion, leads to union with God:

> He [Krishna] is the Supreme Person attainable only through
> Bhakti, in whom all creatures have their being, the One on whom
> all that there is depends.

In that union God becomes known as Bhagavan, Supreme Lord, the Giver of a completely generous love, evoking a corresponding love in return. Those who respond in love are known as Bhagavatas. The exhilaration of that love is expressed powerfully in *Bhagavata Purana*, which tells of the many ways in which Vishnu has become manifest: Bk.10 exemplifies 'the pizza effect' gathering traditions about Krishna; and Bk.11 contains instructions on how the Lord should be correctly worshipped:

Near me is my Lord, beyond time, the One who is the truth of love: in him is delight and completion, all the wealth that I could ever desire.

The union is seen also in the relation between Vishnu and his consort Shri, 'the Gracious' (grace-giving). Shri as Goddess appears in many forms and is worshipped independently, but in union with Vishnu she is such an inseparable part of him that Vishnu bears on his body an indelible mark called Shrivatsa. Devotion to the 'two-as-one' led to a distinct Sampradaya (tradition) known as Shrivaishnavism.

Shiva

Shiva, whose worship is widespread, is a particularly good example of the pizza effect, of existing characterizations of God spreading and being assimilated, and thus changed. The cult of Shiva seems to have begun in the Himalayas before spreading through the whole of India. Shiva scarcely appears in the Vedas except, as we have seen, as an epithet of Rudra (who otherwise is a fearsome and terrifying figure), describing him as 'auspicious'. By the time of the Upanishads, Shiva has displaced Rudra (the Upanishads are a profound exploration of the inner meaning of the Vedic tradition known as Vedanta, and are Shruti or Revelation in Indian understanding: exact dates are uncertain, but roughly 600 BCE onwards). In *Shvetashvatara Upanishad*, Shiva is identified with Rudra (so that Rudra is a name by which Shiva is addressed), and Shiva is the supreme One to whom even Brahma and Vishnu are subordinate—for Shaivites this Upanishad is as revered and sacred as is *Bhagavadgita* for Vaishnavites:

Rudra is absolutely One without any second, who has control over all worlds with his controlling power.... That One has an eye on every side, a face on every side, an arm on every side, a foot on every side: he creates the heavens and the earth, binding them together

with his arms and wings.... Rudra, your embodiment is auspicious
[*shiva*], unterrifying and without evil: with that auspicious body,
O you who dwell among the mountains, be present among us. O
you who dwell among the mountains, make auspicious the arrow
which you hold in your hand ready to throw. You, the Protector
from the mountain, do not harm humans or any living creatures.

As Shiva became supreme he assimilated the way in which Rudra
in *Rig Veda* is manifest through destructive natural forces and is
therefore to be feared, and Shiva can certainly be destructive. But
now Shiva can also direct and control those forces (beneficially
for those who worship him), and he is still rightly known as 'the
Auspicious One'. He is 'the Fearful and Auspicious One', the lord
of death and yet also the origin of life.

The power of Shiva, as that passage from the Upanishad suggests,
is expressed through so many symbols that they become a visible
index of the characterization of God. In the same way, Shiva
is worshipped through many representations and forms of
embodiment (*murti*). A well-known example is that of Shiva as
Nataraja, the Lord of the Dance of time and creation, who both
sustains and destroys the universe: in one hand he holds a drum
summoning the universe into being, in the other he holds a flame
destroying it; the surrounding circle of flames is energy in its
strongest form, but it is also the fire of cremation (see Figure 6).

Among the many symbols, the Linga is supremely important. The
Linga is the penis, the male organ of generation, and it is often
found in temples in association with the Yoni, the female
counterpart, and together they condense into a symbol the
fundamental power that brings all things into being.

In South India, Shiva, like Vishnu/Krishna, became the focus of
Bhakti, producing, amongst much else, the supreme poetry of
devotion of the 63 Nayanmars ('leaders' or 'guides', from the 6th
century CE onwards). According to a popular saying, 'No words can

6. Shiva dancing on Apasmara, the dwarf of ignorance. Accompanying him are sages and Deities including Ganesha, Brahma, and Vishnu in the Avatara form of the Boar

move those who do not melt when they hear these hymns.' It produced also its own Sampradayas, notably Shaiva Siddhantha ('the final truth of Shiva') and the Virashaivites ('heroes of Shiva'). The latter are also called the Lingayats because their only ritual symbol is a Linga worn round the neck: it makes their body a temple so that wherever they go they are always in the presence of God.

Shiva, like Vishnu, has his own Avatars but they are not as decisively important for Shaivites as are those of Vishnu for Vaishnavites. Also like Vishnu, Shiva has his consorts, but in relation to Shiva they are the source of his activity and power. Thus Shakti, divine energy, enables Shiva to create; Parvati, the daughter of the Mountain, enables him to sustain order and peace; Kali, the supremacy of Time, enables him to destroy. Without them, Shiva can do nothing, and therefore in crucial ways he is subordinate to them.

Mahadevi

...Or subordinate to *her* (in the singular), because in this understanding the One source and origin of all being, including devas and gods and goddesses, is Mahadevi, Great Goddess. Monotheism is here more precisely monotheasm (in the feminine). She is the Ruler of the Cosmos (Bhuvaneshvari) and the source of all energy, Shakti. Those who worship her are therefore known as Shaktas. The male gods derive their strength from her, and without her as Shakti they are impotent. On many occasions they have to plead with her to do for them what they cannot do for themselves. Even the throne on which she sits is supported by the lifeless bodies of Brahma, Vishnu, and two forms of Shiva—Rudra and Ishana—and the seat of the throne is the dead body of another form of Shiva, Sadashiva (as in the poem quoted in Chapter 1). The throne is known as *panca-pretasana*, the seat of the five corpses (see Figure 7).

7. Mahadevi, the Great Goddess, known as Bhuvaneshvari, 'Ruler of the Universe'. She is seated on the Throne of the Five Corpses

Mahadevi and her forms of manifestation as Shakti, the energy of cosmic creation and destruction, are literally powerful in the widespread beliefs and practices known as Tantra (*tantra* may mean 'to grow' or 'to expand', but it is more often taken from words meaning 'to weave' and 'to protect'. Tantra 'weaves together the threads of belief and practice that will lead to Moksha'.) Tantra takes many forms, but fundamentally it understands and uses the body as the vehicle through which the power of the cosmic and divine energy can be activated: it is in and through the body that the intense ecstasy of union with Goddess can be realized. For both Shaktas and Tantrikas, Mahadevi is the One without second:

In me this whole world is woven in all directions....

I am the Lord and the Cosmic Soul; I am myself the Cosmic Body.

I am Brahma, Vishnu, and Rudra, as well as Gauri, Brahmi, and Vaishnavi.

I am the sun and the stars, and I am the Lord of the stars.

I am the various species of beasts and birds, I am also the outcast and thief.

I am the evil doer and the wicked deed; I am the righteous person and the virtuous deed.

I am certainly female and male, and asexual as well.

And whatever thing, anywhere, you see or hear, that entire thing I pervade, ever abiding inside and outside.

There is nothing at all, moving or unmoving, that is devoid of me;

For if it were, it would be a nonentity, like the son of a barren woman.

Just as a single rope may appear variously as a serpent or wreath,

So also I may appear in the form of the Lord and the like; there is no doubt in this matter.

The One and the Many

By now, even the shortest introduction to Indian understandings and characterizations of Goddess/God may seem like a guide to an immense 'palace of varieties', and in a sense that is as it should be. The whole universe is made up of manifestations of Goddess/God offering the opportunity to 'see and worship'. The epiphanies interlock and interchange in what is at first sight a bewilderingly complex way, with a dazzling proliferation of traditions, images and temples. So were the Muslims right to call Indians 'polytheists and worshippers of idols'?

To answer that we have to understand how the many different epiphanies relate to the One source from whom they come. In any one lifetime in the long chain of rebirth, individuals choose the way in which they will devote themselves to God/Goddess. They may join a major Tradition or belong to a particular Temple. They may choose their own deity (Ishtadevata) to whom they devote themselves at least for this life, but they still participate in public rituals and worship addressed to other manifestations of God. In India, it is accepted that other deities and other ways of devotion are equally valid. As it is often put, there are many paths leading to the same goal.

The goal, nevertheless, *is* the same. If one thinks of Indian religion as 'a family of religions', then one can see that no matter how far apart the descendants have spread and how different they have become from each other, they can still recognize that they have a common Ancestor. In many different ways attempts were made in the family of Indian religions to give priority in recognition and worship to the One from whom all the variety comes and to whom it all, in its different ways, points.

A notable attempt to do that was made by Guru Nanak (1469–1539), who used Indian and Muslim names of God as different

ways of pointing to Satnam, the One whose Name is true. The Mul
Mantra, the foundation of Sikh belief, begins *Ik Oan Kar*, 'One
Reality Is, the Name is Truth, Source and Creator'. But his
followers, the Sikhs (the name means 'learner' or disciple), like
Jains and Buddhists, separated from the family and became an
independent religion.

In fact, however, the recognition that there can only be One source
of all the variety is an early and common thread in Indian religion.
We have seen it already in the Primordial Origin in the Vedas, and
in the poetry of the Alvars and Nayanmars: the One seeks us,
through a constant act of grace, in many forms of manifestation,
but cannot itself be described:

> He is beyond our knowledge,
> He is this and not this.
> He comes in the form that those who urgently seek him need,
> And yet that is not his form.

Outside the poetry of liturgy and devotion the philosophers of
India tried to articulate how the One is related to the many—and
the systems of philosophy are themselves also known by that key
word for worship, *darshana*, 'viewpoint', or 'contemplation'.
Udayana could therefore state: 'Logical analysis is rightly called
"contemplation of God", and is indeed worship...'.

But who or what is the One? In *Brihadaranyaka Upanishad*
3.9.1.9, the renowned teacher Yajnavalkya is asked how many gods
there are. He replies, '3,306' (the number addressed in a
particular hymn).

> 'Yes', says his questioner, 'But how many really?' Yajnavalkya replies,
> '33' [a number in the Vedas].
> 'Yes, but how many really?'
> 'Three.'

'Yes, but how many really?'

'Two.'

'Yes, but how many really?'

'One and a half.'

'Yes, but how many really?'

'One.'

'Which is the One?'

'The Breath. He is Brahman. They call him That [*Tat*].'

It is Brahman who is the Primordial One from whom all manifestations and appearances come. The name 'Brahman' is usually thought to come from a root meaning 'to increase', 'to strengthen', and it referred in Vedic times to the power that becomes operative through sacrifice and through ritual chant known as Mantra. Later, Brahman becomes the source of all power and indeed of everything, the unproduced Producer of all that is. Brahman becomes manifest as Ishvara, the supreme Being (known also as Purushottama, Supreme Person) from whom come all the manifest forms of Gods and Goddesses, and with them all the forms of appearance that make up a universe. In *Taittiriya Upanishad* 3.1.1. Bhrgu asks his father to define Brahman. His father replies:

> That from which these beings are born, that by which once born they live, that into which when they die they enter, that seek to know, That is Brahman.

The great philosopher Shankara (788–822) argued that there is nothing other than Brahman: Brahman simply is—without attributes or qualities (*nirguna* Brahman). When, however, Brahman extends itself into manifest appearance through Maya, creative power, it becomes possible to infer something about Brahman—Brahman, that is, with attributes (*saguna* Brahman):

> Of Brahman, that which is, there are two modes, one with manifest form, the other without. These changing and unchanging forms exist in all creatures. The unchanging is transcendent Brahman, the

changing is the entire universe. Just as a fire is fixed in one place and sends forth heat and light, so the entire universe is the energy sent forth from the transcendent Brahman.

It is at this point that people fall into trouble—or rather fall into the ignorance (*avidya*) that blocks their progress to Release: they look at changing appearances and think that they are independently real. That mistake is Maya, but the word is now used in the sense of 'creative mistake' or 'illusion'.

It is through the way of knowledge (Jnanamarga) that confusion and ignorance can be dispelled and people can return to the realization that they are *already* Brahman and that in truth they have never been anything other: 'You are That', one of the Great Sayings (known as Mahavakya) which summarize the truth that if there is nothing other than Brahman, then the inner self (Atman) cannot be anything other than Brahman: 'This Self is Brahman.'

On that basis, Shankara's system is known as Advaita, non-dualism. Shankara did not eliminate God, since Brahman is manifest in the forms of Ishvara and of Gods and Goddesses to whom people are related in devotion and worship. Other philosophers, however, believed that that relatedness belongs quintessentially to 'what Brahman is'. In contrast, therefore, Ramanuja (*c.*1017–1137), who was himself a Shrivaishnavite, believed that Bhakti and the ecstatic union with God constitute what Brahman essentially is: as consciousness relates to a body and is inseparable from it, and yet is not identical with it, so Brahman relates to selves and their bodies by being inseparable from them and yet not identical with them. Ramanuja's system is therefore known as 'qualified non-dualism', Vishishtadvaita.

Those and many other reflections on the relation between the One and the many endorse diversity and emphasize the generosity of God: it is from God's exuberant delight in diversity and otherness that the entire created order has come into being. Creation is an act of playful joy, *lila*, defined by Radhakrishnan (1888–1975) as 'the joyous exercise of spontaneity involved in the art of creation'.

The epiphanies of God in Indian belief are a part of that spontaneous generosity through which God creates the ways and the forms through which a real meeting can occur. It is not 'polytheism' since there is only One who is God, no matter how many forms there may be through which the One is approached and found. It is not 'idolatry', since the forms and images are not worshipped but (like icons for Christians) are the means through which people pass to a direct encounter with God. Indians do not confuse the signpost with that to which it points—at the end of an act of worship, the sacred diagram is often swept aside and the image is simply thrown away: it is a means to the End. In the End there is only God in whom already we can be completely immersed:

> You are I, and I am You, without difference, as are gold and the bracelet, the ocean and the wave.... You are the ocean, embracing all, knowing and seeing all. How can I, a fish in the ocean, ever perceive the limit of what you are? Wherever I look, there you are. If I leave you, I gasp and I die.

Chapter 7
On knowing and not knowing God

> Thus it was that on the ninth day of February, at the
> beginning of the thaw, this singular person fell out of infinity
> into Iping village.

So begins chapter 3 of the novel by H. G. Wells, *The Invisible
Man*; the story of a man who finds a way to make himself
invisible. But he had an immediate problem: how can he
communicate with ordinary people if they cannot see him? They
can see his *effects*: when he arrives in London, in Oxford Street,
two urchins see his muddy footprints. 'See 'em?' said one. 'See
what?' said another. 'Why—them footmarks—bare. Like what you
makes in mud.' A crowd follows the footprints but of course they
cannot see him.

Without clothes, and without money to buy any, he remains
invisible. One night, in desperation, he breaks into a shop, seizes
some clothes and pulls them on. In the morning, people do see
him standing in the shop and they react: 'And then, down the vista
of the counters, came a bawling of, "Here he is!"'

This book began with the invisibility of God, not, of course, with
God as the invisible *man* because God is far beyond gender and is
certainly not 'a man'. Still, the fact remains that God cannot be

introduced to you in a visible way, as strangers were introduced to Mr Pickwick, because God is not an object among other objects, able to be seen—or, as the Christian theologian Eriugena (John Scotus, 9th century), put it, 'Even God does not know *what* he is because he is not any what.' Not surprisingly, therefore, the author of the medieval *Cloud of Unknowing* (4) concluded:

> God cannot be comprehended by the intellect of humans or for that matter of angels, for both are created beings. But God is incomprehensible to our intellect only....

To that extent (and breaking off the sentence at that point) God is invisible, as theistic religions have always insisted: 'No one has seen God at any time' (*I John* 1.18); 'His form [*rupa*] cannot be seen: no one sees him with the eye' (*Shvetashvatara Upanishad* 4.20); 'Aisha said, "If anyone tells you that Muhammad has seen his Lord, he is the greatest of liars, for God says [s.6.103], 'No eye can encompass God: God, the invisible [*latif*, too fine to be seen], sees all'"' (Muslim, *alJami al-Sahih*, 1.78.337).

But in that case we are surely right to ask, How on earth can God be known? How *on earth* can God be known? It could only be if God creates the means of that knowing, and of that being known. God therefore can be known, or at least abductively inferred, through the effects 'on earth' that are a consequence of God. They will not be literal footsteps in the snow or the mud, but metaphorically, as the Psalmist put it (in the paraphrase of William Cowper), 'He plants his footsteps in the sea, And rides upon the storm.' To put it in the language of *The Invisible Man*, God has broken into the world and seized the clothes which those with eyes to see *can* see. And then down the vistas of the world come, not the bawling, but the prayers and praises of adoration and worship, saying, 'There God is!'

What, then, are the clothes that make God real to our sight? Or to put it less metaphorically, what are the effects through which God becomes known? To answer that would make an extremely long list, but some of the most widely shared (though not all of them appear in each religion) are gathered in three groups of particular importance.

The first of 'the clothes' is 'the apparel of creation', the beauty, order, reliability, vastness of the universe—and we have seen already how in different ways (or at least in different languages) the philosophers and the poets—and believers in general—recognize God in that clothing. The Quran, for example, speaks of creation full of signs (*ayat*, the same word that is used of the verses in the Quran) that point to God:

> Surely in the creation of the heavens and the earth, and in the
> alternation of night and day, are signs for people who have
> understanding...[when] they think seriously about creation.

It is in the consistency and in the beauty of the universe that we learn to recognize unmistakably the absolute values of truth, beauty, and goodness. The values are absolute in the sense that they are what they are no matter how different are the changing and contingent circumstances in which they happen to occur: 'Euclid alone has looked on Beauty bare....'

Nature thus becomes a text of revelation because from that non-contingency of values (i.e., transcending circumstance) we can begin to recognize the Absolute and non-contingent source from whom they come. As Hepburn put it earlier (see Chapter 2), it is 'the distinctive experience of God as the primary source of beauty and love'. It is the discernment of God in and through the effects, and it is in that way that Francis Thompson began his well-known poem:

> O World Invisible, we view thee,
> O World intangible, we touch thee,
> O World unknowable, we know thee,
> Inapprehensible, we clutch thee!...

The angels keep their ancient places; —
Turn but a stone, and start a wing!
'Tis ye, 'tis your estrangéd faces,
That miss the many-splendoured thing....

The simplicity of a stone—or of mud, as Eck observed in
Chapter 6—as the opportunity of revelation and discovery is an
illustration of the way in which God is widely believed to take
on the clothing of very specific and particular things in creation
in order to become a real and effective presence. Jesus, as we
have seen, took bread and wine to enact the promise of his
presence; Krishna took *ghee*—and a flute. These tangible forms
of enactment are commonly called 'sacraments'. The Latin word
sacramentum meant originally a civil suit or process in the law
courts, and from the solemn promise made in court to tell the
truth, the word came to mean the oath of loyalty sworn by new
recruits to the Roman army; and from that, *sacramentum*
became any kind of solemn commitment or engagement. It is
the kind of promise that parents make to children who are
becoming impatient, exactly as the Roman poet Horace wrote in
Odes 2.17.10: 'Non ego perfidum: dixi sacramentum; ibimus,
ibimus': 'I'm not deceiving you: I said *sacramentum*: we will go,
we will go.'

The word *sacramentum* was for the Romans a word of absolute
promise and commitment, and that is why it was taken up in
early Christianity to express God's commitment in enacted
ways to be present and to make a difference in human lives. A
sacrament is defined in Christianity as 'an outward and visible
sign of an inward and spiritual grace'. Equivalents appear in
other religions, as, for example, in India in what are known as
samskaras. They are called by Pandey 'Hindu Sacraments' (in
the sub-title of his book): they are the rituals and actions
undertaken 'for sanctifying the body, mind and intellect of an
individual, so that he may become a fully fledged member of the
community'.

The second of the ways in which God is 'clothed' (i.e., is discerned) is through the interactive enterprise with humans that is referred to as 'inspiration'—whether in arts or sciences or technologies or in the ways we care for each other. They are the *continuing* works of creativity. If the metaphor of 'clothes' is retained it might be represented through the cloak ('the enfolding cloak where darkness yields to light') in which prophets like Elijah or Muhammad wrapped themselves in order to be hidden with God and in-spired.

Those 'clothes' are thus God's cooperation with humans who are open to the Immanence of God—open, that is, to the difference that God can make. They come from a collaboration between the human and the divine. Both those words, 'cooperation' and 'collaboration', mean literally (from the Latin) 'working together with', and they point to the endless and often astonishing consequences that would not otherwise occur as they do. Humans become secondary agents in the continuing creativity of God.

In a more specific way, inspiration and revelation have often been associated with particular words of which God is believed to be the source and author (working with the agency of particular humans), and which therefore have authority. Even so, we have to remember (as we saw earlier in Chapter 2) that Revelation in one religion may be contradicted by Revelation in another, and that the characterizations of God in any one Revelation change through the process of time with the earlier often being displaced by the later. Nevertheless, the words of Revelation are eloquent of God in enduring ways, not least as they continue to move and inspire people to live and speak of God with confidence and trust.

The third set of 'the clothes' that God has seized in order to become visible takes us back to the 'invisible man' of H. G. Wells and the moment at which 'this singular person fell out of infinity into Iping village'. The clothes are the garments of human flesh in which the singularity of God falls out of infinity and Transcendence into the village of Bethlehem (in the case of Jesus), or of Mathura (in the case of Krishna), or of Ayodhya (in the case of Rama). They are ways in which God is believed (not, of course, by all religions, and emphatically not by Muslims) to have become manifest in human form and through which God continues to reach into the world—and that is why Thompson's poem (above) ends as it does:

> But (when so sad thou canst not sadder)
> Cry;—and upon thy so sore loss
> Shall shine the traffic of Jacob's ladder
> Pitched betwixt Heaven and Charing Cross.
> Yea, in the night, my Soul, my daughter,
> Cry,—clinging Heaven by the hems;
> And lo, Christ walking on the water,
> Not of Genesareth, but Thames!

Those 'epiphanies' (to use the word already explained) might be loosely grouped together as 'the Incarnation of God', but what is believed about Jesus is very different from what is believed about Krishna and Rama: the understanding of the human nature in which each appearance is made is very different, as it is of the human predicament from which they offer a rescue (or rather, different rescues) that humans could not achieve without that help.

They do, nevertheless, share in common that it is God who takes the initiative to meet humans half-way inviting them to receive the help they need. There is much in the human case that needs rescue and repair: '"We all of us have flaws", said the Duke of Coffin Castle, "And mine is being wicked."' The Quran, as we have already seen, has more than a hundred different words for human fault or sin. In *Bhagavadgita* (4.7–8) Krishna declares, 'Whenever Dharma declines and Adharma flourishes, then I manifest myself: for the rescue of the good and the destruction of the evil, for the sake of establishing Dharma, I am born from age to age.'

So why only halfway? Why not the whole way? Because that would be a coerced and unavoidable relationship which would destroy the utterly different quality of what is called in psychology, 'gap-induced relatedness'. What that means is that we close the gap between ourselves and others according to the circumstances we are in and the ways in which we evaluate who 'the others' are and what they are about. If 'the other' is a doctor or nurse, we allow the gap to be closed professionally, even to the extent of our nakedness being disclosed. We close the gap in the company of the one whom we love to the point, not just of nakedness, but of becoming one flesh.

What the Epiphany and epiphanies of God make manifest is the initiative of God in closing the gap between the Creator and the created, so that if we respond it can result in a relatedness of complete disclosure and love. That is why so much of the language and poetry of the human relatedness to God is expressed in terms drawn from the experience of sexuality and of complete love (body, mind, and spirit) between two people—the experience of ecstasy, of being drawn completely out of oneself into union with the other (the Greek words *ek* + *stasis* mean 'standing outside of'). Creation is commonly understood as *God's* ecstasy, God's overflowing into otherness in the exuberant delight that Indians call *lila*. In one of the Hadith Qudsi God declares, 'I was a hidden treasure that I wished to be known, so therefore I created the world.'

When we are invited (but never compelled) to respond to the initiative of God, the gap is completely closed and the result is, as Ruusbroec put it (see Chapter 1), 'an active meeting and a loving embrace', 'a divine state of blissful enjoyment', 'an eternal state of rest in a blissful embrace of loving immersion'.

That ecstatic union of love leads to many different and often extremely practical outcomes—to the selfless sharing of that love with others, for example. There may, however, be times when it seems that God has withdrawn and gone AWOL—absent without leave or any sign of where God is. But those to whom that happens cannot deny or forget the blissful and loving embrace. So even in the darkness and desolation of the absence of God, they do not give up but persist in a condition of trust. This faith in God even in the absence of God is known in India as 'absence-devotion' (Virahabhakti): Jayadeva's Radha 'suffers from the pain of being parted from Krishna':

Like the burning flame
of the fire of passion
her deep sighs
radiate heat.
Her eyes shed tears
like dew from lotuses
with broken stems.

In John of the Cross, in Christianity, the pain of separation, reflecting the pain of Christ on the Cross (see Figure 8), is known as 'the dark night of the soul': 'Beloved, where have you hidden? I went in search of you, but you were gone.' What he and Jayadeva and countless others have found is that continuing trust leads to light and to love:

O lamps of fire bright-burning
with splendid brilliance, turning
deep caverns of my soul to pools of light!
Once shadowed, dim, unknowing,
now their strange new-found glowing
gives warmth and radiance for my Love's delight.

The experience of Love's delight is so memorable, even in the absence of God, that we can now complete the sentence of *The Cloud of Unknowing* the beginning of which was quoted earlier, 'God cannot be comprehended by the intellect of humans,...but God is incomprehensible to our intellect only, never to our love.'

8. This drawing of the suffering Christ was made by John of the Cross. It evoked from Salvador Dali his famous painting 'Christ of Saint John of the Cross' to celebrate the theme of Christus Victor

Never to our love. But love does not mean that we now know everything there is to be known about God. In fact, to be with God and to rest in that blissful embrace leads us into *unknowing*, into the realization that we cannot *know* God, even in the fairly limited way that Mr Pickwick knew his friends. The Muslim cry, *Allahu Akbar*, means literally 'God is greater': whatever we say or think about God must always end with the equivalent words so common in Christian history, *Deus semper maior*, 'God is always greater' than anything we can say or imagine.

That is why, in the end, philosophers can suggest good reasons to conclude *that* God is, but they cannot describe literally *what* God is. Many have therefore concluded that they can only say with confidence what God is *not*. God is not, for example, 4 feet high and 3 feet wide. 'God is not a body, not an object, not a mass, not a form, not flesh, not blood', reported alAshari of another Muslim theologian, who then went on to add a further 60 negatives.

It is true, of course, that much can be said (and *is* said) about God on the basis of 'the clothes that God wears', the effects of God in the Book of Nature and the Book of Revelation; and much also is said and done on the basis of experience of God. That is why philosophers and poets (with whom this book began) are speaking in different ways but with a common voice. This way of speaking positively about God is known as 'kataphatic theology' (from the Greek *kataphasis*, a positive or affirmative statement); and on the same basis believers in general say much in their hymns and prayers. It comes from that well-tested and well-winnowed reliability discussed earlier.

But what God *is* cannot be known, for all the reasons that we have already seen. In that particular sense God *is* unknowable, so that whatever we attempt to say positively about God has to be corrected and indeed negated because it must necessarily always fall short—*Deus semper maior*. Religions recognize this in different words—in Judaism *ayn*, 'nothingness', in Christianity *via negativa*, 'the negative way', in Islam *bila kayf*, 'without knowing how', in India *neti, neti*, 'Not that! Not that!' (or even just, 'No! No!').

The *via negativa* in any of its forms is emphasizing that if we desire and hope to draw closer to God, it will be necessary to abandon our *ideas about* God and realize that none of our concepts will be any use in helping us to describe what God is. In contrast to kataphatic theology, this way of negation is known as apophatic theology, and its truth and importance is found in all theistic religions. According to Eckhart (*c.*1260–1327/8), a daring exponent of apophatic theology, we cannot say that God is 'good' or 'wise' or even that God exists because such words trap the entirely Transcendent God within the limits of our understanding:

> Now pay attention to this. God is nameless for no one can either speak of him or know him.... If I say that 'God is good', this is not true.... 'Good', 'better', 'best', are far from God, for God is wholly transcendent.... Or if I say that 'God exists', this is also not true. He is being beyond being: he is a nothingness beyond being.... Be silent therefore, and do not chatter about God, for by chattering about him, you tell lies and commit a sin.

It follows unmistakably that the *via negativa* is not being in the least negative about God. It is affirming that God is constant invitation, drawing us deeper into love the more we abandon our own ideas and preconceptions.

That is the deepest level at which our own existing 'characterizations of God' have to be changed, abandoned, and displaced—as they have been constantly changed in the history of religions. The more profoundly one enters into that relatedness of love, the more impossible it becomes to put the Other into words: one can only know the condition of love.

That is what Ruusbroec meant when he wrote of 'the fathomless, modeless being of God, so dark and so devoid of particular form', of 'dark stillness in which all lovers lose their way', and of 'the abyss of the ineffable'. It is to enter 'the cloud of unknowing' and to try, as the author of that work put it, 'to pierce that darkness above you, and smite upon that thick cloud of unknowing with a sharp dart of longing love.' Even then the cloud will not vanish:

For when you first attempt it, you find nothing but a darkness, and as it were a cloud of unknowing. All you know is that you feel in your will a naked intent upon God. No matter what you do, this darkness and this cloud is between you and your God, and it hinders you from seeing God clearly by the light of understanding in your reason, and from feeling God in the sweetness of love in your affection. So therefore face up to resting in this darkness as long as may be, always crying after God whom you love. For if ever in this life you see God or feel God, it must always be in this cloud and in this darkness.

This is where any introduction to God, short or long, is leading. We have done as the King of Hearts told us in the first words of of Chapter 1, and we have come to the end. But we cannot obey his final instruction, '…then stop'. We cannot do so because, while we have come to the end of this book, we have also come to the End, the final resting place of all our longing and of all our desire. That is why we find that this is, after all, only the beginning, the start of a new life.

God is invitation, and that invitation is extended to all. If we wish to take it up, how do we do so? We begin with prayer. It starts in extreme simplicity: we come simply and deliberately before God, into the awareness of God. 'You made me and You sustain me. This breath and this moment is Your gift. You know me. Help me to know You.' And since it is a relatedness of love, it will for certain flow over into prayer and into action for others. Even then, it is only a beginning.

Publisher's Acknowledgements

We are grateful for permission to include the following copyright material in this book.

'Our sole duty'...From Indira Viswanathan Peterson, translator and editor. *Poems to Siva: The Hymns of the Tamil Saints.* © 1989 Princeton University Press. Reprinted by permission of Princeton University Press.

'In me this whole world is woven': Reprinted by permission from *The Devi Gita: The Song of the Goddess: A Translation, Annotation and Commentary* by C. Mackenzie Brown, The State University of New York Press © 1998, State University of New York. All rights reserved.

'Like the burning flame'...*Gitagovinda* 4.9.13f., trans. D. Mukhopadhyay, *In Praise of Krishna: Translation of Gitagovinda of Jayadeva*, Delhi, B.R. Publishing, 1990, p.41.

'O lamps of fire': Reproduced by kind permission of the Carmel of Mary and Joseph, from *Centred on Love: The Poems of St John of the Cross*, translated by M. Flower, Varrowville, The Carmelite Nuns, 1983.

'God is not a body': From alAshari, *Maqalat alIslamiyin*, ed. H. Ritter, Istanbul, 1929-30, I, 155f.

All biblical quotations are taken from *The New Oxford Annotated Bible, New Revised Standard Version*, Edited by M.D. Coogan, M. Z. Brettler, C. Newsom, and P. Perkins (Oxford University Press, 2010).

God

References

Books that may be helpful as Introductions are marked*.

Preface

A bunch of squabbling prima donnas...T. Griffith and H. Griffith, *Ancient Greek Philosophy: An Introduction*, Naxos Audio Book, 2007.

In its infinite mystery...J. Hick, 'A Response to Cardinal Ratzinger on Religious Pluralism', *New Blackfriars*, LXXVIII, 1997, p. 457.

Chapter 1: Does God exist?

The White Rabbit...L. Carroll, *Alice's Adventures in Wonderland*, ch. 12.

Some large being...Augustine, *The Confessions*, 1.9.14; when he was older he asked, 'Of what was I thinking when I said, "God"? A certain great and perfect Being which transcends every changeable creature of flesh and spirit...., a certain Being, living, eternal, omnipotent, infinite, everywhere present, everywhere whole, nowhere confined...' (*Homilies on the Gospel of John*, 1.1.8).

How is the claim...? R. Swinburne, *The Christian God*, Oxford: Clarendon Press, 1994, p. 125.

The year of grace 1654...Pascal's Memorial.

Our sole duty...Appar in I. V. Peterson, *Poems to Śiva: The Hymns of the Tamil Saints*, Delhi: Motilal Banarsidas, 1991, p. 295.

The Newtonian universe...M. Kumar, *Quantum: Einstein, Bohr and the Great Debate about the Nature of Reality*, London: Icon Books, 2010, p. 218.

A favourite problem . . . Letter to Herbert Spencer, *Life and Letters of Huxley*, I, p. 231.

The only thing . . . R. Feynmann, 'First Principles of Quantum Mechanics', in *Easy and Not-So-Easy Pieces*, London: Folio Society, 2008, p. 113.

If and only if it is impossible . . . C. Taliaferro, *Consciousness and the Mind of God*, Cambridge: Cambridge University Press, 1994, p. 287.

Someone tells us . . . A. G. N. Flew, ed., *New Essays in Philosophical Theology*, London: SCM, 1955, p. 98.

The god hypothesis . . . D. Bonhoeffer, *Religion without Revelation*, pp. 58, 62; *Letters and Papers from Prison*, London: Collins, 1953.

That eternal and infinite Being . . . B. de Spinoza, *Ethics*, in C. Gebhardt, *Opera*, Heidelberg: Winters, 1925, IV, p. 206.

Animism is . . . E. B. Tylor, *Primitive Culture*, London, 1871, I, p. 426.

The name . . . P. Tillich, *The Shaking of the Foundations*, London: Penguin, 1962, p. 63f.

The Father . . . J. Ruusbroec, *The Adornment of the Spiritual Marriage*, trans. C. A. Wynschenk, London: Dent, 1916, p. 173.

Now this active meeting . . . *John Ruusbroec: The Spiritual Espousals and other Works*, trans. J. A. Wiseman, Mahwah: Paulist Press, 1985, p. 152.

Udyana defended . . . N. S. Dravid, *Nyayakusumanjali of Udayanacarya*, Delhi: Indian Council of Philosophical Research, 1996.

Science qua science . . . *A. Flew, *There Is a God: How the World's Most Notorious Atheist Changed His Mind*, New York: HarperCollins, 2007, p. 155.

We shall be rationally warranted . . . J. Foster, *The Divine Lawmaker: Lectures on Induction, Laws of Nature and the Existence of God*, Oxford: Clarendon Press, 2004, p. 160.

Richard Dawkins on the question 'Why': see J. Bowker, *The Sacred Neuron*, London: I. B. Tauris, 2005, p. ix.

The fact of the matter . . . *B. Davies, *Thinking about God*, London: Chapman, 1985, p. 28.

There are no good philosophical arguments . . . D. Conway, *The Rediscovery of Wisdom*, London: Macmillan, 2000, p. 134.

Chapter 2: Why believe in God?

The purpose of the Holy Spirit . . . Galileo, 'Letter to the Grand Duchess Christina', ed. M. A. Finocchiaro, *The Galileo Affair: A*

Documentary History, Berkeley: University of California Press, 1989, p. 96.

They did this... Polybius, *Histories*, VI, §56.

Śruti [Scripture] is the final authority... S. M. S. Chari, *Advaita and Viśiṣṭādvaita: A Study Based on Vedanta Desika's Śatadūṣaṇi*, London: Asia Publishing House, 1961, p. 78ff.

Each piece... R. Feynmann, *Easy and Not-So-Easy Pieces*, London: Folio Society, 2008, p. 4.

The origin of consciousness... J. Jaynes, *The Origin of Consciousness in the Bicameral Mind*, new edn., London: Penguin, 1993.

As long as our brains... *A. Newberg, E. d'Aquili, and V. Rause, *Why God Won't Go Away*, New York: Ballantine, 2001, p. 172.

Spiritual awareness... *D. Hay, *Something There: The Biology of the Human Spirit*, London: Darton, Longman and Todd, 2006, p.xii.

A sort of mystic illumination... B. Russell, *The Autobiography of Bertrand Russell*, London: Unwin Books, 1975, p. 149.

Was radiated... K. Clark, *The Other Half*, London: John Murray, 1977.

The distinctive experience... R. W. Hepburn, 'Holy, numinous, and sacred', in T. Honderich, ed., *The Oxford Companion to Philosophy*, Oxford: Oxford University Press, 1995, p. 372b.

It [belief] changes with them... J. H. Newman, *Development of Christian Doctrine*, 1.1.5.7.

There are people... C. J. Jung, Foreword to V. White, *God and the Unconscious*, London: Harvill, 1952, p. xiii.

Dawkins singled out... In the Preface to the paperback edition of *The God Delusion*, Dawkins stated (London: Black Swan, p. 15) that there are 'subtle and nuanced' forms of religion that would make the world a better place, but that his targets were those whose characterizations of God are *not open to change* or challenge. In fact his attack is more general but for reasons of space cannot be considered here. The serious errors in Dawkins' account, not just of religion but also (more surprisingly) of genetics and evolution, are examined in more detail in J. Bowker, *Why Religions Matter*, Cambridge: Cambridge University Press, 2014.

Chapter 3: The religions of Abraham: Jewish understandings of God

As for the towns...: *Deuteronomy* 19. 16–8.

Now therefore revere... *Joshua* 24. 14–5.

Then the fire... *I Kings* 18. 21–40.

In the year... *Isaiah* 6.1; cf. *Amos* 9.1, 'I saw the Lord standing beside the altar...'.

He shall make atonement... *Leviticus* 16.16.

God is One... Maimonides, *Fundamental Principles of the Torah*, 1.

Know therefore... *Deuteronomy* 7. 9–11.

Thus says God... *Isaiah* 42. 5–9.

Thou shalt survive. For this and a summary of other Jewish responses to the Holocaust, see *The Oxford Dictionary of World Religions*, 'Holocaust, Shoah, Hurban'.

Solly Gitnick... This poem, derived from an incident described in William McAllister's *A Handful of Rice*, is in J. Bowker, *Before the Ending of the Day*, Toronto: Key Publishing, 2010, p. 23.

No group or nation... D. Runes, *The War Against the Jew*, New York: Philosophical Library, 1968, p. 82.

Chapter 4: The religions of Abraham: Christian understandings of God

Father, hallowed be your name... *Luke* 11.2; there is a longer version in *Matthew* 6.9f.

You shall love... *Matthew* 22. 37–40.

Trinitarian theology... *C. M. LaCugna, *God for Us: The Trinity and Christian Life*, New York: HarperCollins, 1991, p. 243.

Do we worship...? *M. Wolf, *Do We Worship the Same God?* Grand Rapids, MI: Eerdmans, 2012.

Chapter 5: The religions of Abraham: Muslim understandings of God

The Quran is the speech of God... *AlFiqh alAkbar II*, art.3: for this and other so-called 'creeds': see *W. Montgomery Watt, *Islamic Creeds: A Selection*, Edinburgh: Edinburgh University Press, 1994.

The best act of worship... *W. C. Chittick, *Sufism: A Beginner's Guide*, Oxford: Oneworld, 2008, p. 67.

If there is a single word... *M. Ruthven, *Islam: A Very Short Introduction*, Oxford: Oxford University Press, 2000, p. 49.

D. Thomas, *Anti-Christian Polemic in Early Islam: Abu 'Isa al-Waraq's 'Against the Trinity'*, Cambridge: Cambridge University

Press, 1992; as an edition of the text, this is not in itself introductory, but the Introduction gives a clear account of the many different understandings among Christians of God and of Christ that Muslims encountered.

Man's self-sufficiency...W. Montgomery Watt, *Free Will and Predestination in Early Islam*, London: Luzac, 1948, p. 165.

All things that people do...*AlFiqh alAkbar II*, art.6.

The [rulers] have an obligation...Ziya udDin Barani, *Tarikh-i-Firuzshahi*, ed. A. Khaan, Calcutta: Asiatic Society of Bengal (Bibliotheca Indica, 32), 1860–2.

Chapter 6: Religions of India

There is nothing...*D. L. Eck, *Encountering God: A Spiritual Journey from Bozeman to Banaras*, Boston: Beacon Press, 1993, p. 83. Note also Eck, *Darśan: Seeing the Divine Image in India*, Chambersberg: Anima Press, 1981.

Puja is the ceremonial act...*S. Huyler, *Meeting God: Elements of Hindu Devotion*, New Haven: Yale University Press, 1999, p. 36.

Come, Dawn...*Rig Veda* 7.77.

I [Vac]support...*Rig Veda* 10.125.

They call it...*Rig Veda* 1.164.46.

The pizza effect: A. Bharati, 'The Hindu Renaissance and its Apologetic Patterns', *Journal of Asian Studies*, XXIX, 1970, p. 273.

Early Buddhism...M. M. J. Marasinghe, *Gods in Early Buddhism: A Study in Their Social and Mythological Milieu as Depicted in the Nikayas of the Pali Canon*, Kelaniya: University of Sri Lanka, 1974, p. 79.

Look! You can see...*Tiruvaymoli* 5.2.1.

He [Krishna] is the Supreme Person...*Bhagavadgita* 8.22.

Near me is my Lord...*Bhagavata Purana* 11.3.

Rudra is absolutely One...*Shvetashvatara Upanishad* 3. 2–6.

In me this whole world...*Devi Gita* 3.12–8, trans. C. M. Brown, *The Devi Gita: The Song of the Goddess*, Albany: State University of New York Press, 1998, p. 118.

He is beyond our knowledge...*Tiruvaymoli* 2.5.9.

Of Brahman, that which is...*Vishnu Purana* 1.22.

Logical analysis...Udayana, *Nyayakusumanjali* 1.3.

Chapter 7: On knowing and not knowing God

Surely in the creation...Quran 3.185/188; cf. the longer list of signs in 2.159/164.

Euclid alone...E. St. V. Millay in *American Poetry, 1922: A Miscellany*, New York: Harcourt, Brace, 1922.

O world invisible...Francis Thompson, *Selected Poems of Francis Thompson*, London: Burns, Oates, 1921, p. 132f.

For sanctifying the body...R. B. Pandey, *Hindu Samskaras: A Socio-Religious Study of the Hindu Sacraments*, Benares: Vikrama, 1949.

Like the burning flame...*Gitagovinda* 4.9.13f., trans. D. Mukhopadhyay, *In Praise of Krishna: Translation of Gitagovinda of Jayadeva*, Delhi: B. R. Publishing, 1990, p. 41.

O lamps of fire...M. Flower, trans., *Centred on Love: The Poems of St John of the Cross*, Varrowville: The Carmelite Nuns, 1983, p. 18.

God is not a body...alAshari, *Maqalat alIslamiyin*, ed. H. Ritter, Istanbul, 1929–30, I, 155f.

Now pay attention to this...Sermon 28, in O. Davies, trans., *Meister Eckhart: Selected Writings*, London: Penguin, 1994, p. 236f.

For when you first attempt it...*The Cloud of Unknowing*, 3.

Further reading

A *Very Short Introduction* to God is dealing with a vast—some might say infinite—subject, and virtually every sentence is open to question or challenge. There are other voices to be heard. Nevertheless, it may be helpful to know that some of my own books go into further detail and contain longer bibliographies than is possible here. Note in particular:

God: A Brief History, London, Dorling Kindersley, 2002: this traces the diverse understandings of God down to the present.

The Message and the Book, London, Atlantic Books, 2011: this offers a more detailed introduction to the sacred texts of the major religions including those discussed or mentioned in this book.

The Sense of God: Sociological, Anthropological and Psychological Approaches to the Origin of the Sense of God, 2nd edn, Oxford, OneWorld, 1995: details of research have moved on, but it still provides a background and context to current debates.

Some of the books included in the section on References are well-suited to further reading of an introductory kind. They are marked with an asterisk, *, and only the author and title are repeated here.

On the opening chapters

The opening page raises the issue of 'male' and 'female', and of gender-specific language, in relation to God: there are good discussions of this in the Christian context in: A. F. Kimel ed., *Speaking the Christian God: The Holy Trinity and the Challenge of Feminism*, Grand Rapids, Eerdmans, 1992; and G. M. Jantzen, *Power, Gender and Christian Mysticism*, Cambridge University Press, 1995, is an excellent example of the application of a feminist perspective to a central topic.

*B. Davies, *Thinking About God*; more recently he has written *The Reality of God and the Problem of Evil* (London, Continuum, 2006) in which he addresses the question raised in Chapter 1.

R. Swinburne, *The Christian God*, Oxford, Clarendon Press, 1994; this is not introductory, but he attempted a more accessible summary in *Is There a God?*, Oxford, Oxford University Press, 1996.

*A. Flew, *There Is a God*.

On Aquinas and Udyana

E. Feser, *Aquinas: A Beginner's Guide*, Oxford, Oneworld, 2009.

There is no equivalent introduction to Udyana of which I am aware. The nearest, but not easy, is:

G. Chemparathy, *An Indian Rational Theology: Introduction to Udyana's* Nyayakusumanjali, Leiden, Brill, 1972.

Neuroscience and experience

*A. Newberg, E. d'Aquili and V. Rause, *Why God Won't Go Away*.

*D. Hay, *Something There: The Biology of the Human Spirit*.

On the Abrahamic Religions

F. E. Peters, *The Children of Abraham: Judaism, Christianity, Islam*, Princeton University Press, 2004.

M. Byrne, *The Names of God in Judaism, Christianity, and Islam: A Basis for Interfaith Dialogue*, London, Continuum, 2011.

*M. Wolf, *Do We Worship the Same God?* Note also his *Allah: A Christian Response*, New York, HarperOne, 2011.

J. Imbach, *Three Faces of Jesus: How Jews, Christians, and Muslims See Him*, Springfield, Templegate, 1992.

On Jewish understandings of God

L. Jacobs, *A Jewish Theology*, London, Darton, Longman and Todd, 1973; note also his *Hasidic Prayer*, London, Littman Library, 1993.

J. Magonet, *The Explorer's Guide to Judaism*, London, Hodder and Stoughton, 1998.

I. Clendinnen, *Reading the Holocaust*, Cambridge, Cambridge University Press, 1999.

On Maimonides

J. S. Minkin, *The World of Moses Maimonides*, New York, Yoseloff, 1957.

On Christian understandings of God

P. Vardy and J. Arliss, *The Thinker's Guide to God*, N. Arlesford, O Books, 2003.

S. J. Grenz and R. E. Olsen, *20th Century Theology: God and the World in a Transitional Age*, Denvers Grove, Paternoster, 1992.

J. P. Mackey, *The Christian Experience of God as Trinity*, London, SCM, 1983.

*C. M. LaCugna, *God for Us: The Trinity and Christian Life*.

G. W. Hughes, *God of Surprises*, London, Darton, Longman and Todd, 1985.

On Muslim understandings of God

Further reading

K. Cragg, *Readings in the Quran*, Brighton, Sussex Academic Press, 1999.

K. Cragg and M. Speight, *Islam from Within: Anthology of a Religion*, Belmont, Wadsworth, 1980.

*M. Ruthven, *Islam*.

*W. Montgomery Watt, *Islamic Creeds: A Selection*.

M. Akyol, *Islam without Extremes: A Muslim Case for Liberty*, New York, Norton, 2011; this offers, from a Hanafite (explained in his book) perspective, a lucid and well-informed account of the historical divisions among Muslims in the understanding of what 'obedience to God', i.e., Islam, must mean.

M. A. Quasem, *Salvation of the Soul and Islamic Devotions*, London, Kegan Paul, 1983; a summary of obligations in relation to God.

On Sufis

*W. Chittick, *Sufism: A. Beginner's Guide*.

On alGhazali

W. Montgomery Watt, *Muslim Intellectual: A Study of Al-Ghazali*, Edinburgh, Edinburgh University Press, 1963.

On Rumi

A. Harvey, *Light upon Light: Inspiration from Rumi*, Berkeley, North Atlantic Books, 1996.

On Indian understandings of God

G. Flood, *An Introduction to Hinduism*, Cambridge, Cambridge University Press, 1996.

A. Daniélou, *Hindu Polytheism*, London, Routledge, 1964; in this summary of the major manifestations of 'God' in India, Daniélou explains carefully in the introduction how 'polytheism' is to be understood in an Indian context.

K. K. Klostermaier, *Hindu Writings: A Short Introduction to the Major Sources*, Oxford, Oneworld, 2000.

*D. L. Eck, *Encountering God: A Spiritual Journey from Bozeman to Banaras*.

Much of the Indian understanding of God is expressed in non-verbal, often physical, form—note, therefore, Huyler *Meeting God*, in the References. See also:

H. Elgood, *Hinduism and the Religious Arts*, London, Cassell, 1999.

A. Shearer, *The Hindu Vision: Forms of the Formless*, London, Thames and Hudson, 1993.

In the Image of Man: The Indian Perception of the Universe through 2000 Years of Painting and Sculpture, London, Arts Council of Great Britain, 1982; this is the Catalogue of the exhibition held at the Hayward Gallery in 1982 as part of the Festival of India: it is well illustrated with informative text.

On knowing and not knowing God

J. Bowker, ed., *Knowing the Unknowable: Science and Religions on God and the Universe*, London, I. B. Tauris, 2009; not all the contributions are introductory, but of those that are, note especially: B. McGinn, 'Three Forms of Negativity in Christian Mysticism' G. Flood. 'Knowing the Unknowable in Indian Traditions' and on God and poets: M. Bowker, 'The Unknowable Not Unknown: The Poetry of R. S. Thomas', F. X. Clooney, 'Divine Absence and the Purification of Desire: A Hindu Saint's Experience of a God Who Keeps his Distance'.

On John of the Cross

I. Matthew, *The Impact of God*, London, Hodder and Stoughton, 1995.

On Eckhart

R. Woods, *Eckhart's Way*, Dublin, Veritas, 2009; this is developed further in *Meister Eckhart: Master of Mystics*, London, Continuum, 2011.

Index

SOCIAL MEDIA
Very Short Introduction

Join our community

www.oup.com/vsi

- Join us online at the official Very Short Introductions **Facebook** page.
- Access the thoughts and musings of our authors with our online **blog**.
- Sign up for our monthly **e-newsletter** to receive information on all new titles publishing that month.
- Browse the full range of Very Short Introductions online.
- Read **extracts** from the Introductions for free.
- Visit our library of **Reading Guides**. These guides, written by our expert authors will help you to question again, why you think what you think.
- If you are a teacher or lecturer you can order inspection copies quickly and simply via our website.